MW00488484

MODERN CROCHET

MODERN CROCHET

PATTERNS & DESIGNS FOR THE
MINIMALIST MAKER

Written + designed by Teresa Carter, Founder of DeBrosse
Foreword by Alexandra Tavel

paige tate
& CO.

Copyright ©2019 by Teresa Carter

Published by Blue Star Press
PO Box 8835, Bend, OR 97708
contact@paigetate.com
www.paigetate.com

Photography | Alexandra Tavel + Nick Hoge

ISBN 978-1944515850

Printed in China
12 11 10 9 8 7 6 5

FOR OUR
TWO LITTLE BOYS

✕

Nou renmen nou deja.

38

62

80

120

INSIDE

FOREWORD

If the idea of crochet conjures up images of old ladies in wingback armchairs stitching multicolor granny square blankets with a cat curled up at their feet, *Modern Crochet* is here to shatter this stereotype and dispel everything you thought you knew about the craft.

It's been nearly three years since I met Teresa ("T") at a crowded Whole Foods in Columbus Circle to talk shop, and I'm still hanging on her every word. The truth is, even as an established knitwear designer myself, I had fangirled over T's modern, sophisticated approach to crochet and knitting and was thrilled to be meeting someone else with a young, fresh perspective on age-old fiber arts. Since this first meeting, I've watched Teresa transition from an Etsy seller of handmade goods to a consummate authority on the business of this industry, and she's become a dear friend and advisor along the way.

I'm continually impressed by T's remarkable ability to take even the most complicated concepts—be it words, designs, directions, or ideas—and restructure them in a way that is all at once digestible, succinct, eloquent, and articulate. She has mastered the art of simple sophistication, both in the designs she creates and her ability to teach others, and this book is the culmination of her gifts.

Modern Crochet is unlike any fiber arts book I've come across. In addition to offering an incredible array of beautiful, functional designs, this book contains the most thorough breakdown of crochet terminology, skills, and pattern reading tips available, which makes it approachable for a complete beginner. It's the kind of book I wish existed when I was first learning, and one that I find endlessly inspiring even as an advanced crocheter. Comprehensive, innovative, and coffee table-worthy, *Modern Crochet* is truly a book for all.

Still fangirling,
"Two"

—Alexandra Tavel, @TwoofWands

#MYMODERNCROCHET

INTRO

I learned to crochet so that I could make blankets for children growing up in the orphanages of Haiti after the 2010 earthquake. One of my first blankets went to a bright-eyed four-year-old boy named DeBrosse. His friendship forever changed the way I see the world. I founded the DeBrosse brand in 2013, and annually set aside a portion of all proceeds to help fund needs at his orphanage, as well as business loans for Haitian women. By supporting my work, you are supporting many others.

Living in New York City, I am surrounded by a modern, minimal, and neutral lifestyle that is not represented in the craft space. I began designing and innovating to bridge this gap through my work. DeBrosse is now a full-service knitwear brand, challenging the status quo of the crochet aesthetic. After selling thousands of individually hand-crafted pieces, I transitioned to selling the patterns to my work, and ultimately created an entire Masterclass on exactly how I built a business against the grain.

Every time I sat down to work on this book, I reflected on my own learning experience, and imagined the dream resource I wish I had at day one, and the one I wish to consult in my office today. For first-time crocheters, I recalled the things that held me back, that made the craft seem intimidating and unappealing, and the teaching techniques that helped me learn the most. For seasoned crocheters, I reflected on all the hacks that I felt differentiated my work, the resources that I consult time and time again, and the ways I pivot and add nuance to existing skills to get more modern results.

It is my hope that this book meets you exactly where you are, and equips you for where you want to go. I made every effort to create a comprehensive learning and design experience, replacing the often fractured learning process with a thoughtful workflow. This book is composed of three sections: Fundamentals, Patterns, and Stitches + Skills.

In **Fundamentals**, I'll walk you through how to pick out your tools and materials, like we're at the craft store together. I'm then going to take you deep into the world of pattern language, so grab a glass of pinot, because we'll need a minute.

The real fun begins as we enter the **Patterns** section, housing 16 unique projects, each named after a Haitian city. This collection features modern stitches, classic textures, chic finishes, and no frills. They are listed in no particular order, so jump around and dive in where inspired. Each pattern begins with a full list of featured stitches and skills, complete with reference page numbers for a quick and easy refresh. Most patterns include step-by-step photos as well as video tutorials, designed to increase your ease and confidence. *Oh*, and I don't particularly enjoy projects that take nineteen Saturdays to complete, or require a great deal of counting, so I won't be asking that of you either.

The **Stitches + Skills** section is your comprehensive reference guide, not only for patterns in this book, but patterns everywhere. It includes step-by-step written instructions, photos, and videos for the primary building blocks of crochet.

As you work through the book, please take advantage of the *Modern Crochet* online video library. It features video tutorials for both stitches and project-specific nuances, full reference charts for hook sizes and pattern abbreviations, and shoppable links for all featured tools and materials. Enjoy your private access to debrosse.com/moderncrochet with password: mymoderncrochet.

I can't wait to see the colors you choose, and the way you grow as a maker. Tag me on Instagram @debrosse_nyc, and use the hashtag #mymoderncrochet so we can do this together.

♡T

FUNDAMENTALS

YARN

INTRO

The patterns in this book are designed with a variety of yarn weights, price points, brand names, and fibers. We'll dive into projects on normal yarn, multi-ply cotton, wool, alpaca, roving, velvet, faux fur, and more. While working with each of them, you'll quickly become fond of certain kinds over others, notice fun nuances that different types of yarn provide, and figure out which ones you appreciate most.

My goal is to provide you with a range of opportunities to explore the material possibilities, and ultimately form your own opinions. There is of course, no right or wrong preference when it comes to yarn.

When working through the patterns in this book, I recommend first making each project on the featured yarn to ensure accuracy. However, after you get the hang of a project, I highly encourage you to go rogue and make adjustments to the pattern and materials to reflect your own style. After all, one of the best parts of handcrafting is that you can create *exactly* to your own liking.

Picking out the yarn is easily my favorite part of any project, and in this section I'll walk you through how to confidently do just that.

SHAPE

HOW TO USE

Yarn is often packaged into one of the following finished shapes: skeins (rhymes with grains), balls, hanks, or cakes. The shape has nothing to do with the yarn itself, but does determine how you work with it. The ideal scenario is that your yarn effortlessly comes out of the *center* of its packaging, allowing the yarn to remain stationary as you work.

A **Skein:** (far right) The skein is oblong in shape, and the most common shape of yarn found at larger retailers. You'll quickly locate a tail end on the outside of the skein, but it should be ignored. Instead, reach into the center from one end, pull out a handful of yarn, and locate the interior tail end. Start here.

Ball: (bottom middle) The ball looks like a flattened ball, and is not as widely available as the skein. To use, insert both fingers into the center of the ball and pull out a portion of the yarn in order to locate the interior tail end. Start here.

Hank: (top middle) The hank is a beautifully twisted formation of yarn, more commonly found in local yarn stores or higher-end boutiques. While beautiful, it's actually the most impractical shape, as working with it will result in a tangled mess. To use, the hank will first need to be spun into a cake, which is often done at the point of purchase.

Cake: (far left) The cake is cylindrical in shape, and though it can be purchased this way, it is often a shape used to wind hanks or scrap yarn. To use, reach into the center of the ball to locate the interior tail end. Start here.

SIZE

YARN WEIGHT

Despite its name, yarn weight actually has nothing to do with physical weight. Yarn weight refers to the thickness of the yarn, and is arguably the most important factor when choosing project materials. Weight categories range from zero to seven, with zero being the thinnest, and seven the thickest. In addition to a number, each category has a name, as well as yarn types that fall within that category.

WEIGHT	CATEGORY	TYPES
0	Lace	Lace, Crochet Thread
1	Super Fine	Sock, Fingering, Baby
2	Fine	Sport, Baby
3	Light	DK, Light Worsted
4	Medium	Worsted, Afghan, Aran
5	Bulky	Chunky, Craft, Rug
6	Super Bulky	Bulky, Roving
7	Jumbo	Jumbo, Roving

All the projects in this book use weights three through six. These weights are easily accessible, affordable, and work up quickly. When purchasing your yarn, simply check the label (or product description, when ordering online) for the yarn weight.

ENDS

JOINING NEW YARN

Most projects require more than one skein (ball, hank, or cake) of yarn. When joining, it is important to leave *at least* a 4" tail on both ends of the yarn for weaving in later. To transition, simply tie a square knot by working right over left, then left over right. Work the knot close to the base of the stitch, and whenever possible, on the wrong side of the work.

WEAVING IN ENDS

Almost every project will wrap up with the instruction to weave in ends. Ends are any piece of yarn that is protruding from the work, including the beginning tail end, the ends of any joined yarn, and the final tail end. The tool used to weave is called a darning needle, which is just like a normal sewing needle but much larger and not as sharp.

To weave in ends, slip an end on the darning needle, slide *through* adjacent stitches in one direction, and then back the other way. Working both directions helps ensure the ends won't pop out over time. There are no right or wrong stitches to go through because every pattern will have more and less conspicuous ways of hiding the yarn.

COLOR

UNIQUE FEATURES

In addition to every color you could ever want, there are a few nuances that provide an additional level of visual interest. Here are a few of my favorites:

A **Tweed:** Tweed is a solid color yarn featuring specks and flecks of different fibers and colors worked throughout. It is rich in texture and nuance.

B **Heather:** Heathered yarn has monochromatic color variation that creates a subtle but rich depth, giving it more interest than a pure solid.

C **Marled:** Marled yarn consists of multiple colors of yarn spun together to create an almost candy-cane striping effect within the yarn itself.

D **Variegated:** Variegated, sometimes called self-striping yarn, changes color over yardage. This gradation adds great visual interest to otherwise simple designs, and is often seen as having a surprise effect, as it's hard to anticipate exactly what it will look like when worked up.

+ **Tip:** When a palette of yarn includes colors with these nuances, they sometimes come with fewer yards per skein, even though they look identical to the solid colors. For this reason, review yardage carefully.

DYE LOTS

Manufacturers dye yarn in batches, which are considered to have near perfect color consistency. It is industry best practice to check dye lot numbers listed on the label when purchasing for a project. (That being said, I would not lose sleep over it if, to your eye, the skeins look and feel the same.)

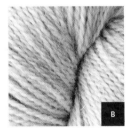

TOOLS

CROCHET HOOKS

MATERIALS

Crochet hooks come in a variety of materials, with the primary options being plastic, bamboo, and aluminum. I recommend spending time with each type of tool to get a sense for its pros and cons. Over time, you'll find that you may prefer certain materials at certain sizes, or for certain types of projects. Like yarn preferences, there are no right or wrong answers here.

A **Plastic:** (back right) Plastic hooks are made in all the common sizes, including jumbo. They are lightweight, smooth, and inexpensive.

Bamboo: (back left) Bamboo hooks are also lightweight, warm to the touch, but the smoothness will vary by manufacturer. While beautiful, wooden tools can slow down the making process (though this may be preferred if the yarn is especially slippery). They are not often available (nor do I recommend them) in the smallest sizes.

Aluminum: (front middle) Aluminum hooks are available in a wide range of sizes, excluding jumbo. These hooks are smooth, cool to the touch, and their slippery surface allows for quicker stitching.

SIZE

Crochet hooks come in a standard set of sizes, always measured in millimeters, and often assigned a corresponding letter and number.

So how do you know which size you'll need? Patterns will always list this information. If, however, you're designing your own project, the yarn label will have a recommended hook size. I would use that as a general guideline (+/- mm) and not a hard-and-fast rule.

US HOOK SIZES

mm	Letter/Number
2.25 mm	B-1
2.5 mm	
2.75 mm	C-2
3.125 mm	D
3.25 mm	D-3
3.5 mm	E-4
3.75 mm	F-5
4 mm	G-6
4.25 mm	G
4.5 mm	7
5 mm	H-8
5.25 mm	I
5.5 mm	I-9
5.75 mm	J
6 mm	J-10
6.5 mm	K-10½
7 mm	
8 mm	L-11
9 mm	M-13
10 mm	N-15
11.5 mm	P-16
12 mm	
15 mm	P/Q
15.75 mm	Q
16 mm	Q
19 mm	S
25 mm	T/U/X
30 mm	T/X

HOW TO READ A PATTERN

LANGUAGE

INTRO

Patterns can be written by any maker, anywhere. (*You could write your own pattern by the end of this book!*) In order to ensure consistent pattern writing across the board, writers adhere to a universally accepted set of abbreviations, terms, and punctuation used within a particular framework. This book is written using standard US terms.

As is the process with picking up any language, it comes with a learning curve. Once you're familiar with the vocabulary and structure, you'll be autonomous in both your reading and potential writing of patterns.

This section is designed to cover the information needed to complete all the patterns in this book, but also to set you up for future success in reading patterns from other writers. To do so, I will often indicate the various ways an instruction might be written. I love a good analogy, so think about this as if I were going to teach you how to greet a friend. I might suggest you say "Hey!" while also recognizing that others prefer "Hi" or "Hello" and those are both acceptable and generally mean the same thing. Don't feel the need to memorize every variation, as I will stick to a single variation throughout the book, but know that this content is available for later reference.

STRUCTURE

Below are the categories of language elements that make up standard pattern language, as well as a few common examples. A full chart can be found on p. 34.

Stitch abbreviations: Every stitch is reduced to an abbreviation.

ch	chain
sc	single crochet

Terms: The most common crochet instructions are written in terms. Terms are either an abbreviated version of a word, or a single word standing in for an entire phrase.

rep	repeat (do the instruction again)
turn	turn your work to start a new row

➕ **Note:** For easy reference, pattern writers often preface a pattern with a legend of stitch and term abbreviations used in the pattern.

Punctuation: In addition to using abbreviations and terms, standard pattern language utilizes common punctuation marks like asterisks *, brackets [ ], and parentheses ( ). These marks serve as shorthand for more verbose instructions, like repeats and groupings. The proper usage of these punctuation marks is explained on p. 30.

➕ **Note:** More advanced patterns can include symbols and/or charts. While I don't cover that content in this book, the abbreviations and terms covered will prepare you to understand the vast majority of patterns on the market.

SLIP KNOT

The slip knot is a technique used to attach the yarn to your hook. This is the very first step of almost all patterns, so much so that it is often implied and not even listed in the instructions. (See p. 142 for how to make a slip knot.)

CHAIN

After attaching the yarn to your hook with a slip knot, you'll crochet a foundation to build the work. This foundation is made up of chain (ch) stitches. (See p. 144 for how to make a chain.) The pattern will indicate exactly how many to make, either *as part of* row 1 (Example 1), or *preceding* row 1 (Example 2). Both mean the same thing.

Example 1   Row 1: Ch 20; sc in 2nd ch from hook and in each ch across. (19)

Example 2   Ch 20.
Row 1: Sc in 2nd ch from hook and in each ch across. (19)

Count your chains as you go, and double-check your final count before moving on to the next step. Note that the loop on your hook does *not* count.

➕ **Tip:** A pattern *may* start off with something like "multiple: an even number of sts," or "multiple: 10 sts + 6." The multiple is used only when deviating from the designer's final size, and ensures that the chain foundation has the appropriate proportion of stitches to match the work. An even number of stitches means the pattern will work whether you chain 4 or 128, but not if you chain 17. The multiple of 10 sts + 6 is any multiple of 10 (10, 50, 110), plus 6 (so 16, 56, 116).

ROW 1

You've completed your 20 chain foundation, and the pattern goes on to say sc in 2nd ch from hook and in each ch across. (19). In conversational terms, here is what is happening:

Sc: Sc is the abbreviation for single crochet, which is the stitch you will use until instructed otherwise. (See p. 148 for how to single crochet.)

2nd ch from hook: This refers to the placement of your very first stitch.

A Count the first and second chain coming off your hook (remember, the loop on your hook doesn't count). Do nothing with the chain you counted as one, and insert your hook into the second chain. (It's almost impossible to stitch into the very first chain off your hook anyway, so this step will come more naturally than it sounds.)

in each ch across (and sometimes, in back bump): This language indicates *where* you should work the first row of single crochet stitches.

B To work "in each ch across," insert your hook through the following loops. (This is most common.)

C To work "in back bump," first rotate the chain toward you, then insert your hook through the following loops. (This creates a slightly cleaner edge. Back bump is sometimes referred to as ridge.)

(19): This number serves to confirm the total number of stitches made on that row, and is *not* a new step. When double-checking your row stitch count, do not count the loop on your hook as a stitch. The total stitch count may also be written as: (14 sc), : 14 sts, —14 sts, 14 total sts, <14sc>, **14**, or *14*. Additionally, it may not be listed at all. This is often the case when stitch count doesn't change from the previous round or row.

TURNING CHAIN

Crochet stitches are always worked from right to left unless instructed otherwise, or in the case of left-hand crocheting. At the end of every row, the work needs to be turned (with your hook still in it), so you can continue working from right to left. In order to make this transition between rows, a pattern will call for a turning chain, written as <u>ch 1, turn.</u> It may fall at the end of a row (Example 3), or the beginning of the next row (Example 4). Both mean the same thing.

Example 3 Row 1: Sc in 2nd ch from hook and in each ch across; <u>ch 1, turn.</u> (19)
Row 2: Sc in each st across; <u>ch 1, turn.</u> (19)

Example 4 Row 1: Sc in 2nd ch from hook and in each ch across. (19)
Row 2: <u>Ch 1, turn;</u> sc in each st across.

This is the same chain technique used in the foundation, but as the name suggests, it is paired with a turn. Adding a chain between rows establishes the proper height needed for your next row. (For taller stitches, the turning chain may require 2, 3, or 4 chains, but a pattern will always indicate exactly how many.) When counting the total number of stitches for a row, the turning chain will not count as a stitch unless the pattern indicates otherwise.

➕ **Tip:** When working a pattern structured like Example 3, note that there is no need to complete a turning chain after the *final* row of a project. This is assumed knowledge, and thus not always indicated within the pattern. If indicated, it might sound like <u>omit turning chain after final row/round.</u>

ROWS

BUILDING + IDENTIFYING

Work will sometimes have a right and a wrong side. In some projects, this will be obvious, and in others it is less so. Regardless, a pattern may refer to an instruction to be completed on a right side (rs) row or a wrong side (ws) row. Additionally, a pattern may give an instruction that is to be applied for all right side (or wrong side) rows.

Example 5   Row 1 (rs): Sc flo in each st across. (19)
             Row 2 (ws): Sc blo in each st across. (19)

➕ **Tip:** If there is no obvious right or wrong side, the right side is considered the one facing you when the beginning tail end is at the bottom left.

Another way of referring to rows is by their even or odd row count. In Example 6, The instruction on the first line is to be applied on rows 1, 3, 5, and so on, up to row 13. The instruction on the second line is to be applied to rows 2, 4, 6, and so on, up to row 14. This is simply a succinct way of consolidating a pattern.

Example 6   Row 1-13 odd: Sc flo in each st across. (19)
             Row 2-14 even: Sc blo in each st across. (19)

In some cases, a pattern may give a goal measurement in addition to or instead of a final row count. This instruction is often given when it's either *more important* that the final measurement be exact (in the case of a sweater sleeve), or when it might simply be *tedious and not integral* to achieve an exact row count (in the case of a blanket).

Example 7   Repeat rows 2-3 twenty times, or until work reaches 60 inches from row 1.

STANDING STITCH

While this is indeed a stitch, I bring it up here because it is a technique used for starting a new row. The standing stitch doesn't get much airtime in crochet, but it is a great skill to have in your bag. Rather than chaining and turning the work between rows, the standing stitch uses a completely new piece of yarn to begin the next row.

A   To create a standing stitch (in pattern, it will indicate exactly which type of stitch, such as standing single crochet), create a slip knot and place yarn on hook. Work into indicated stitch.

In most contexts, this would just be unnecessary work (thus why the skill is not widely known). But in particular projects, it can make all the difference.

B   The Bainet Throw (see p. 120) utilizes the standing stitch to create a texture that cannot be achieved through turning the work.

SHORT ROWS

Short rows are a super simple, but often overlooked, variation on the standard row. To create a short row, you'll simply leave stitches unworked, work a turning chain, then move on to the next row as normal. It will feel and look as if you are ending the row before you actually get to the end of the row. Those unworked stitches are stitched into on a later row, and this pull creates a 3-D effect to the work.

Example 8   Row 2: Sl st blo in first 40 sts, leave remaining 3 sts unworked; ch 1, turn. (40)

C   The Torbeck Beanie (see p. 80) utilizes the short row technique to create a 3-D dome effect for the top of the hat.

ROUNDS

ROUNDS VS. ROWS

So far, we've covered how to crochet in rows and turn at the end of each row to start a new row. This method is great for linear or rectangular pieces like a blanket. But what about something like an infinity scarf or a basket? When you want to work in a circle (whether it's a tube shape or a flat shape), you'll swap *rows* for *rounds*, and the process is called "working in the round." A round is very similar to a row, except that the end of a round will meet the beginning of that same round. (If you think back to the *rows* of a blanket, recall that the beginning and end of a row were on opposite sides.)

There are three ways to join a round: continuous rounds, joined rounds, and joined turned rounds. A pattern will indicate which method(s) to use. In all methods, it is best practice to place a stitch marker (abbreviated pm for place marker) into the first stitch of every row in order to most easily recognize it when getting to the end of the round.

- **Tip:** I *always* think I'll remember where the first stitch was...but I *never* do. Use the stitch marker.

- **A** Crochet stitch markers have an opening, allowing the marker to slide directly into a stitch. A safety pin or scrap piece of yarn will also do the trick.

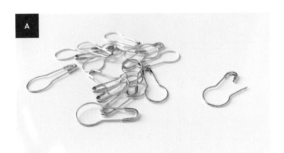

JOINS

CONTINUOUS ROUNDS

With continuous rounds, there is no true transition between rows (e.g., a chain or a slip stitch), and the effect is something like a spiral. You'll work the first stitch of your next round into the first stitch of the previous round. Continuous rounds are one of the most effortless ways to crochet, as there is no turning or joining.

JOINED ROUNDS

Joined rounds have a definitive beginning and end (unlike continuous rounds). At the end of each round, it is connected to the beginning of that same round with a join (often in the form of a slip stitch) to complete the round. This join is most often worked into the first stitch or the first chain, and the pattern will specify.

To create the height to begin the next round, the pattern will call for a chain (or multiple chains, depending on stitch height). This chain acts like the turning chain of rows, but when working in rounds, you won't turn the work. A joined round will have a slightly visible seam because of the slip stitch and chain.

JOINED TURNED ROUNDS

Joined turned rounds are just as they sound: a joined round that *does* include a turn. At the end of each round, it is connected to the beginning of that same round with a join to complete the round. Then, a full turning chain is made. A joined round will have a slightly visible seam because of the slip stitch and chain.

SHAPES

BUILDING SHAPES IN THE ROUND

Despite its name, a round can be used to make angled shapes like squares, triangles, and hexagons. In this book, however, rounds are used to make circular shapes, both in the form of flat, concentric circles, and tube shapes. Picture a basket—the bottom is a flat circle, while the sides are a tube shape. While both shapes are constructed from rounds, utilizing any one of the three joining techniques listed on the previous page, they have unique starting points worth noting.

TUBE SHAPE

The tube shape begins similar to a project constructed from rows, with an initial foundation chain, but followed by an instruction to join. To do so, bring the opposite end around, ensure the chain isn't twisted, locate the first chain, then slip stitch into the chain.

> **Example 9** Begin: With loose tension, ch 88.
> Sl st to first ch to join (careful not to twist); ch 1, do not turn.

If the chain is twisted prior to joining the work, it will create a twist in the work. In most cases, this is an undesirable effect. However, the occasional pattern may intentionally call for a twisted chain, so be sure to follow suit (as is the case with the Gonaïves Faux Fur Cowl on p. 68).

After the foundation is connected, the remainder of the work simply builds upon this completed circle.

FLAT SHAPE

Flat shapes worked in the round often begin with a technique called the magic ring (see p. 162), rather than a foundation chain. The magical aspect of the ring is that it has a slip knot effect that can be pulled taut after the first row of stitches is worked into it (see p. 164).

> **Example 10** Begin: Create a magic ring. Ch 1.
> Round 1: Sc 7 in ring; sl st to join, ch 1. (7)

When constructing concentric circles, each round needs to be larger, by way of additional stitches, than the previous round. To do so, concentric circles require a technique called increases (written as inc in next st), which is to work *multiple* stitches into the *same* stitch (see p. 29). The following example uses the *, which indicates the starting point of a repeated sequence.

> **Example 11** Round 2: Inc in each st; sl st to join, ch 1. (14)
> Round 3: *Sc in next st, inc in next st; rep from * around; sl st to join, ch 1. (21)
> Round 4: *Inc in next st, sc in next 2 sts; rep from * around; sl st to join, ch 1. (28)
> Round 5: *Sc in next 3 sts, inc in next st; rep from * around; sl st to join, ch 1. (35)

There are a few things happening in Example 11:

+ We started with 7 stitches (Example 10, round 1), so the total stitches for each row increases by 7.
+ These additional 7 stitches show up as one additional stitch *between* each increase.
+ The rounds alternate between starting and ending with the increase. This technique staggers the increases to create a more rounded result. (When increases align, the piece takes a "number-gon" look. Eight stitches will result in an octagon, 10 will become a decagon, etc.)

STITCH LOCATIONS

LOOPS

Crochet stitches are worked through *both* loops unless otherwise indicated. This is implied (much like the initial slip knot), and often goes unmentioned. However, beautiful things happen when stitches are worked through only a back or front loop.

A The back loop is always the loop farthest from you, and the front loop is always the loop closet to you, even when the work is turned.

When a pattern calls for a stitch to be worked through the back loop only (bl or blo) or front loop only (fl or flo), the abbreviation will append the stitch to which it applies. In the following example, you will create 3 sc through both loops (because no loop is indicated, it is understood that it's both), then 10 sc through the back loop only, then 3 sc through both loops of the last 3 stitches (again, because no loop is indicated, it implies both).

Example 12 Row 1: Sc in next 3 sts, sc blo in next 10 sts, sc in next 3 sts; ch 1, turn. (16)

SPACES

Some patterns may call for stitches to be skipped. When a stitch is skipped, a chain stitch *may* be made to maintain that space. This technique creates a space underneath the chain where the stitch was skipped, which can be stitched into later. This is called a chain space (ch-sp).

Tip: Note that whenever you see the abbreviation for chain (ch) appended with a hyphen (e.g., ch-sp) it is a noun and not a verb, meaning no stitches are worked, they are simply referenced.

Example 13 Row 1: Sc in 4th ch from hook, *ch 1, sk 1 st, sc in next st; rep from * across row; ch 2, turn. (44)

Row 2: Sc in first ch-sp, *ch 1, sk 1 sc, sc in next ch-sp; rep from * across row; ch 2, turn. (44)

B Arrow points to ch-sp.

C The Limbé Linen Scarf (see p. 114) utilizes this technique.

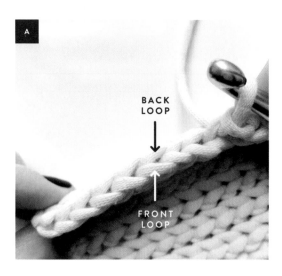

INCREASES + DECREASES

PURPOSE

Increases and decreases are techniques used to grow or reduce the number of stitches in a row or round, and therefore the overall size or shape of a project. Increases and decreases are general terms that are more specifically defined within each pattern.

D The Vache Bolster Pillow (see p. 86) utilizes both increases and decreases in the construction of its circular ends.

INCREASE (INC)

An increase (inc) is where multiple stitches (any number, any kind) are worked into the same stitch. Usually, this means two of the same stitch you've been using up until the increase.

> **Example 14** Round 3: *Sc in next st, inc in next st; rep from * around; sl st to join, ch 1. (21)

DECREASE (DEC)

A decrease (dec) is worked over more than one stitch, where multiple stitches *become* a single stitch.

> **Example 15** Round 3: *Sc in next st, dec in next 2 sts; rep from * around. (21)

In this book, all decreases are constructed by working two single crochets together (which could also be written more specifically as sc2tog). After mastering the single crochet on p. 148, review steps 1–6 to complete a single crochet decrease.

1. Insert hook in next stitch, going under both loops.
2. Yarn over.
3. Pull yarn through stitch to draw up a loop (2 loops on hook).
4. Repeat steps 1–3 (3 loops on hook).
5. Yarn over and pull yarn through all 3 loops on hook.
6. This completes 1 decrease.

PUNCTUATION

OVERVIEW

In addition to abbreviations and terms, pattern language utilizes common punctuation marks like asterisks, brackets, and parentheses. These marks serve as shorthand for more verbose instructions, like repeats and groupings.

ASTERISKS *

Crochet projects are built from a series of stitches, oftentimes in a repetitive fashion. Repeats (rep) may occur from row to row, or within a row itself. Instead of writing out the same instruction multiple times, asterisks are used to indicate these large-scale repeats.

There are two ways asterisks may be used in a pattern, both indicating a repeated sequence. The repeated sequence may live *after* an asterisk (Example 16), and the instruction will say rep from * across. Or, the repeated sequence may live *between* two asterisks (Example 17), and the instruction will say rep from * to * across. In either example, the instructions after or between the asterisks, respectively, are repeated until the row is completed. Anything before or outside the asterisks, respectively, is not repeated.

Example 16 Row 3: Sc in first st; *bo in next st, sc in next st, rep from * in each st across. (19)

Example 17 Row 3: Sc in next 3 sts; *ch 1, skip next st, sc in next st*, rep from * to * in each st across. (19)

Note that the instruction in each st across may be written in a variety of ways, all meaning the same thing:

+ in remaining stitches (in rem sts)
+ all stitches (all sts)
+ till end of row (rep till end of row)

To provide greater specificity, the asterisk can also be followed by the number of times the segment should be repeated. When an asterisk precedes a repeat, the maker stitches it first, *then* repeats it the indicated number of times (Example 18). Designers may also choose to be more overt in indicating this by saying rep from * 4 *more times* (Example 19).

Example 18 Row 1: Ch 1, *sc in next st, dc in next st; rep from * 4 times. (10)

Example 19 Row 1: Ch 1, *sc in next st, dc in next st; rep from * 4 more times. (10)

PARENTHESES ( ) + BRACKETS [ ]

Parentheses and brackets can be used to indicate a variety of instructions. Each application is largely contextual, and can be understood based on its location and/or surrounding language. Below is a list of applications and their respective meanings. You'll notice that parentheses are used more often than brackets, but in some cases, they are interchangeable.

Total stitches: As mentioned in earlier examples, a stitch count listed in parentheses at the end of a row indicates the total stitches to be completed on that row.

> **Example 20** Row 1: Sc in all sts. (19)

Repeats: Much like the asterisk, both the parentheses and brackets can indicate a repeated sequence. Unlike the asterisk, parentheses and brackets are followed by the *total* number of times the sequence should be stitched.

> **Example 21** Row 1: Ch 1, (sc in next st, dc in next st) 5 times. (10)

> **Example 22** Row 1: Ch 1, [sc in next st, dc in next st] 5 times. (10)

Clarification: Just as parentheses are used in everyday writing to provide clarification, they may be used that way in a pattern. This is where a pattern can go from feeling like alphabet soup to feeling like you're sitting in a coffee shop with a friend.

> **Example 23** Row 1: Place ring over yarn, then yo and draw through loop on hook. (This completes 1 sc.)

Working multiple stitches into a single stitch: Most often, each stitch is worked into a stitch by itself. In some instances, multiple stitches are worked into a single stitch. To indicate this, the grouping of stitches is placed within parentheses, never brackets, and *immediately prefaced or appended by* language like in next st. The pattern may be even more specific and say in next sc, which means the same thing, but is simply providing greater clarity. Be careful to recognize when the instructions are calling for a single crochet to be worked, versus stitched into.

> **Example 24** Row 1: (hdc, ch 1, hdc) in next st.

Multiple sizes: A pattern may include instructions for multiple sizes, and will use parentheses to organize stitch counts. This is most commonly found in garment patterns and will always be prefaced by a note indicating how the numbers within parentheses correspond to each respective size.

> **Example 25** Pattern is written for multiple sizes showing stitch counts as follows: S (M, L).
>
> Row 1: Sc 20 (24, 28), hdc in next 3 sts; ch 1, turn. (23 (27, 31) sts)

Note that the final stitch count is expanded to represent total stitches for each respective size.

> ● **Tip:** When working on a pattern with multiple sizes, it is immensely helpful to first go through and highlight all stitch counts that pertain to the size you are making.

MANAGING GAUGE

TENSION

If you and I both sit down and crochet 100 stitches, chances are, our work will be slightly different lengths. This is the result of how tight we each perform our stitches, which is referred to as tension. Tension naturally varies between makers and can produce unintended consequences (like a three-quarter sleeve that was meant to be a long sleeve). Gauge is a concept designed to help account for this.

Gauge measures the number of stitches and rows per inch. For the most accurate reading, gauge is most often provided for a 4" x 4" (10cm) square, unless indicated otherwise. A pattern will indicate gauge up front, allowing you to make an *optional* test swatch (a practice referred to as swatching) to check your tension against that of the pattern and make any necessary adjustments before starting. You do not *have* to do this (I rarely do), but the information will be made available for you.

A Sample swatch, made slightly larger than 4" x 4" to measure stitches without including turning chains.

> **Example 26** Gauge: 6 sts x 7 rows
> **Example 27** Gauge: 4 sts x 8 rows in pattern
> **Example 28** Gauge: 10 sts in pattern x 12 rows

⊕ FYI: If the gauge contains the language in pattern, it's recognizing that not all stitches or rows use a single stitch, and instead refers to the *repeat* as seen in the pattern.

ADJUSTING

If the gauge is off, your finished piece will end up either shorter or longer than the finished dimensions indicated in the pattern. Getting the perfect finished size is most important when it comes to worn garments and accessories.

➕ **Tip:** When I'm working on a project like a blanket or bin, where the final size is arbitrary, I just throw on Netflix and tell myself it will be close enough. For most patterns in this book, that will be the case.

Rows are less important to match when measuring gauge, as you can simply add or subtract rows as you work. If your stitches are off, here's how to adjust:

+ If you have *more* stitches per inch than the pattern calls for, use a *larger* size hook.
+ If you have *fewer* stitches per inch than the pattern calls for, use a *smaller* size hook.

RESIZING

Gauge can also be proactively used to resize a pattern. Decide how much taller or wider you want your finished piece to be, and consult the gauge for how many additional stitches or rows to work in order to achieve those measurements.

SUBSTITUTIONS

For each pattern in this book, I share the brand, name, color, and weight of the featured yarn. I recommend using the same yarn to ensure accuracy, but you are welcome to review the weight to substitute for an alternative.

It is worth noting that not all yarn within a single weight is identical, meaning that a weight four yarn I use may be slightly off from the weight four yarn that you choose. (To be sure though, a four will always be more similar to a four than a three or a five.) This is largely the result of production method and fiber content variations.

So what's the big deal? Even the slightest variation in thickness will be multiplied across hundreds or thousands of stitches and result in a smaller or larger finished piece. Additionally, it will require a different total yardage than indicated by the pattern. To properly substitute a different yarn (because someday you're going to fall in love with some one-of-a-kind indie artist yarn that begs to be a sweater), be sure to create a test swatch and check your gauge against the listed gauge and adjust accordingly.

MULTI-STRANDED + DOUBLE-STRANDED

To achieve a heavier weight, you have the option to crochet multiple strands of yarn at the same time. This technique is referred to as working the yarn multi-stranded (or double-stranded when specifically referring to two yarns). Below are a few scenarios where you might opt for this method:

+ You love a particular lighter-weight yarn (and/ or simply have it on hand), and want to work a pattern that calls for a heavier weight.
+ You want to create a marled, variegated, or fade effect, and use this method to pair complementary colors together.

There are no universal conversion standards to follow here, outside of trial and error.

🅱 The Vache Bolster Pillow utilizes the double-stranded technique to create a heavier-weight velvet yarn.

ABBREVIATIONS

Below is a list of crochet abbreviations used in patterns by designers and publishers. These definitions reflect standard US crochet terminology. The patterns in this book will only use a portion of these abbreviations.

A	**alt**	alternate
	approx	approximately
B	**beg**	begin/beginning
	bet	between
	bl or blo	back loop or back loop only
	bo	bobble
	BP	back post
	BPdc	back post double crochet
	BPdtr	back post double treble crochet
	BPhdc	back post half double crochet
	BPsc	back post single crochet
	BPtr	back post treble crochet
C	**cc**	contrasting color
	ch	chain stitch
	ch-	refer to chain or space previously made (e.g., ch-1 space)
	ch-sp	chain space
	cl	cluster
	cont	continue

D	**dc**	double crochet
	dc2tog	double crochet 2 stitches together (or any number of stitches)
	dec	decrease
	dtr	double treble crochet
E	**edc**	extended double crochet
	ehdc	extended half double crochet
	esc	extended single crochet
	etr	extended treble crochet
F	**fl or flo**	front loop or front loop only
	foll	following
	FP	front post
	FPdc	front post double crochet
	FPdtr	front post double treble crochet
	FPhdc	front post half double crochet
	FPsc	front post single crochet
	FPtr	front post treble crochet
H	**hdc**	half double crochet
	hdc2tog	half double crochet 2 stitches together (or any number of stitches)

I	inc	increase
J	join	join two stitches together
L	lp	loop
M	m	marker
	mc	main color
P	pat or patt	pattern
	pc	popcorn stitch
	pm	place marker
	prev	previous
	ps or puff	puff stitch
R	rem	remaining
	rep	repeat
	rnd	round
	rs	right side

S	sc	single crochet
	sc2tog	single crochet 2 stitches together (or any number of stitches)
	sh	shell
	sk	skip
	sl st	slip stitch
	sp	space
	st	stitch
T	tbl	through back loop
	tch or t-ch	turning chain
	tog	together
	tr	treble crochet
	tr2tog	treble crochet 2 stitches together (or any number of stitches)
	trtr	triple treble crochet
	turn	turn your work
W	ws	wrong side
Y	yo	yarn over
	yoh	yarn over hook

36

PATTERNS

THE CROIX
COASTER

✕

This modern take on the coaster provides the perfect pop of chic to your coffee table. The clean lines of the stitch are complemented by the curvature of the wooden ring, creating a simple but stunning pairing of materials.

Construction: The coaster is worked with a slip stitch in the back loop only, creating a texture that looks knitted. On the final few rows, we'll leave a few stitches unworked in order to carve out a space for the ring. Leaving stitches unworked is a simple but brilliant technique that can be used for many things, and in this case, shaping. We'll finish the coaster by single crocheting the ring into place.

✕

HOOKS
7 mm
5.5 mm • US size I

YARN
Weight 5 • 50 yds per coaster
Bernat, Maker Home Dec
Color: Cream

OTHER TOOLS
Wooden rings, 2" (1 per coaster)
Darning needle

GAUGE (4x4")
13 stitches x 20 rows

FINAL SIZE
5¾ x 5¾"

PREFACE

The following stitches, techniques, and abbreviations are featured in this project. Take a moment to review before starting.

▶ Video + material support: debrosse.com/moderncrochet

	back bump / p. 22
blo	back loop only / p. 28
ch	chain / p. 144
sl st	slip stitch / p. 146
st(s)	stitch(es)
yo	yarn over / p. 141

BODY

Body is worked with 7 mm hook. Turning chain does not count as st.

	Begin	Ch 20.
	Row 1	Sl st into back bump in 2nd ch from hook and in each ch across; ch 1, turn. (19)
	Rows 2–21	Sl st blo in each st across; ch 1, turn. (19)
A	**Row 22**	Sl st blo in 16 sts across, leaving 3 sts unworked; ch 1, turn. (16)
	Row 23	Sl st blo in each st across; ch 1, turn. (16)
B	**Row 24**	Sl st blo in 15 sts across, leaving 1 st unworked; ch 1, turn. (15)
	Rows 25–27	Sl st blo in each st across; ch 1, turn. (15)
	Finish	Omit the turning chain after final row.
		Cut yarn, and draw through loop on hook. Weave in ends.

RING

Start new yarn.

C Use 5.5 mm hook to work sc into each of the 7 indicated sts, using blo in sts 1–3.

D To begin, insert hook in st 1. Leave 6" tail and place yarn over hook. Draw up a loop.

E Place ring over yarn, then yo and draw through loop on hook. (This completes 1 sc.)

F Sc through remaining 6 sts, working over ring as you make the stitch.

Cut yarn, and draw through loop on hook.

G Rotate sts to the back of your work. Weave in ends.

THE LES CAYES
WALL HANGING

✕

I dreamt up the Les Cayes Wall Hanging in the spring when I still had the itch to crochet, but could not stomach the thought of anything winter-related. I love the texture and lines that it adds to a wall, while still remaining classically simple.

Construction: This piece is worked from the top down, starting with the widest row and working toward the narrowest. The diagonal is created by leaving stitches unworked, specifically the final bobble and single crochet of each row. Bobbles normally pop *away* from you while you work them, but to achieve a right-to-left slant, we'll pop them *toward* us.

After we've completed all the rows, we'll single crochet the work onto the dowel rod, then add our final tassels.

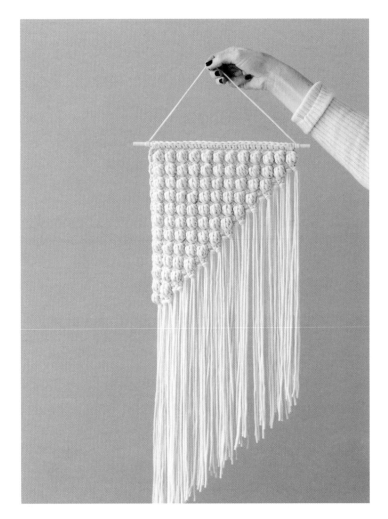

✕

HOOKS

7 mm

5.5 mm • US size I

YARN

Weight 5 • 165 yds

Bernat, Maker Home Dec

Color: Cream

OTHER TOOLS

Dowel rod (12" x ¼")

Darning needle

GAUGE (4x4")

Counting bobbles only:

5 stitches x 5 rows

FINAL SIZE

Not including rod or wall attachment:

Width: 10"

Height: 27"

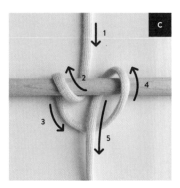

PREFACE

The following stitches, techniques, and abbreviations are featured in this project. Take a moment to review before starting.

▶ Video + material support: debrosse.com/moderncrochet

bo	bobble stitch / p. 158
ch	chain / p. 144
even	even numbered rows (4, 6, 8 … 24)
odd	odd numbered rows (5, 7, 9 … 25)
rep	repeat
sc	single crochet / p. 148
st(s)	stitch(es)

BODY

Wall hanging is worked with 7 mm hook. Turning chain does not count as stitch. Pop bobbles *toward* you while working them.

Begin	Ch 26.
Row 1	Sc in 2nd ch from hook and in each ch across; ch 1, turn. (25)
Row 2	Sc in first st, *bo in next st, sc in next st, rep from * across; ch 1, turn. (25)
Row 3	Sc in each st across; ch 1, turn.
Rows 4–24 even	Sc in first st, *bo in next st, sc in next st, rep from * across, leave 2 sts unworked; ch 1, turn.
Rows 5–25 odd	Sc in each st across; ch 1, turn.
Finish	Omit the turning chain after final row. Cut yarn, and draw through loop on hook. Weave in ends.

ROD

A Using 5.5 mm hook, work 25 sc into foundation chain and around dowel rod to attach. (25)

TASSELS

Each tassel is made up of two pieces of yarn. There are 24 tassels in total, 2 under each bobble stitch along the diagonal edge.

Cut 48 pieces of yarn, 33" each.

B Insert hook from back to front and place 2 pieces of yarn on hook and draw up a loop. Yarn over with all 4 tail ends, and draw through to secure tassel.

Cut 24"piece of yarn.

C Secure to each end of rod with a double half hitch. Weave in ends.

THE ENNERY
TWISTED HEADBAND

×

The Ennery Headband is a winter staple. My hair is in a topknot most days, so I usually prefer a headband to a hat. This design is super simple in texture, with a twist that gives it the perfect amount of chic, without being too bold.

Construction: For this headband, we'll be working lengthwise, in slip stitch back loop only (sl st blo) to create a knit-like look. As always with the slip stitch, it's important to keep a loose tension to make up for its lack of stretch.

The bottom half of this headband is created in basic rows. For the top half, we'll begin a row as normal, then go rogue and begin building a new chain foundation. The second half of the headband will also be basic rows, simply built on the new chain. This will create two long, skinny halves, attached at one end. We'll eventually cross the top half over the bottom to build in the twist. Finally, we'll complete the headband with a whip stitch seam.

X

HOOK
7 mm

YARN
Weight 4 • 90 yds
Lion Brand, Wool-Ease
Color: Natural Heather

OTHER TOOLS
Darning needle

GAUGE (4x4")
12 stitches x 24 rows

FINAL SIZE
After seaming, when laid flat:
Width: 9¼"
Height: 4½"

PREFACE

The following stitches, techniques, and abbreviations are featured in this project. Take a moment to review before starting.

▶ Video + material support: debrosse.com/moderncrochet

	back bump / p. 22
	whip stitch / p. 166
blo	back loop only / p. 28
ch	chain / p. 144
cont	continue
rs	right side
sl st	slip stitch / p. 146
st(s)	stitch(es)

BODY

Headband is worked in rows. Turning chain does not count as a stitch.

Begin	Ch 59.
Row 1	Sl st into back bump in 2nd ch from hook and in each ch across; ch 1, turn. (58)
Rows 2–12	Sl st blo in each st across; ch 1, turn. (58)
A **Row 13 (rs)**	Sl st blo 22 sts, ch 36 with loose tension; ch 1, turn.
Row 14	Sl st into back bump in 2nd ch from hook, and all ch sts. (36) *The 36th chain won't have a back bump, so go through as normal.* Cont in sl st blo to end of row; ch 1, turn. (58)
Rows 15–24	Sl st blo all sts; ch 1, turn. (58)
Row 25 (rs)	Sl st blo 36 sts; proceed to next section. (36)

TWIST

B **(rs)** Cross top half over bottom.

C **(rs)** Cont in sl st blo while also inserting hook through back loops of top half. (22) Cut yarn, and draw through loop on hook.

SEAM

Cut 30" piece of yarn and thread through darning needle, doubled.

D With right side facing out, hold ends together and match up rows. Whip stitch through 2 loops on each side.

| **Finish** | Cut yarn, and draw through loop on hook. Weave in ends. |

THE HINCHE
THROW

✕

The Hinche Throw features a classic ribbed texture that pops right off the blanket. The stitch combo used for this piece creates a heavy fabric, resulting in an almost weighted blanket that you'll never want to come out from under.

Construction: The blanket is worked lengthwise, in rows, alternating between a row of half double crochets and a row of slip stitches. All stitches are worked in the back loop, which creates a ribbed texture that immediately pops up on the right side and is incredibly satisfying to watch. The wrong side is more of a flat weave, with a different, but beautifully dense, texture of its own.

While the slip stitch rows don't create any height, the half double crochet rows compensate for that, giving the blanket a relatively painless work-up time. Due to the unstretchy nature of slip stitches, they should be done with a loose tension.

Alterations: For a longer blanket, chain additional stitches at the beginning. For a wider blanket, work additional rows (always end on a half double crochet row). Remember, you can always consult the gauge to review the exact width and height of stitches and rows.

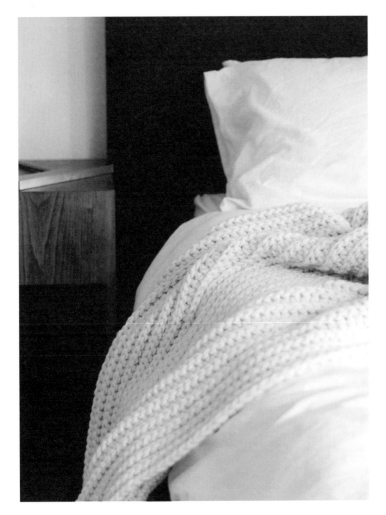

✕

HOOKS
11.5 mm • US size P

YARN
Weight 6 • 975 yds
Lion Brand, Wool-Ease Thick & Quick
Color: Fisherman

OTHER TOOLS
Darning needle

GAUGE (4x4")
7 stitches x 6 rows
(6 rows includes 3 hdc, 3 sl st)

FINAL SIZE
Width: 38"
Length: 54"

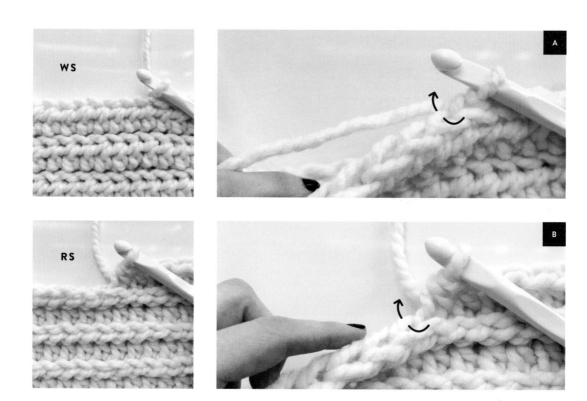

PREFACE

The following stitches, techniques, and abbreviations are featured in this project. Take a moment to review before starting.

▶ Video + material support: debrosse.com/moderncrochet

blo	back loop only / p. 28
ch	chain / p. 144
hdc	half double crochet / p. 150
rs	right side
sl st	slip stitch / p. 146
st(s)	stitch(es)
ws	wrong side

BODY

Blanket is worked lengthwise, in rows. Turning chain does not count as a stitch.

	Begin	Ch 90.
	Row 1	Hdc in 3rd ch from hook and in each ch across; ch 1, turn. (88)
A	**Row 2 (ws)**	With loose tension, sl st blo in each st across; ch 2, turn. (88)
B	**Row 3 (rs)**	Hdc blo in each st across; ch 1, turn. (88)

Repeat rows 2 and 3 until 61 rows are completed.

Finish	Omit the turning chain after final row.
	Cut yarn, and draw through loop on hook. Weave in ends.

THE BELLADÈRE
BOBBLE PILLOW

×

My apologies, in advance, for every guest that comes into your home and must run their fingers across this pillow. The bobbled texture is a showstopper, and is just as much fun to work up as it is to look at.

Construction: The pillow is made in two pieces: a front and back panel, that are seamed together at the end. The front panel features the bobble texture, while the back is a simple single crochet (though, if you're feeling fancy, you're welcome to make two front panels).

The bobble stitch is created by working 5 double crochets together into a *single* stitch, which essentially creates an (adorable) bump. In this pattern, and often elsewhere, each bobble is separated by a single crochet *stitch*, and each bobble *row* is separated by a single crochet *row*. These single crochets aren't visible, but are there to provide appropriate spacing and alignment. Note that the bobbles are staggered. To achieve this, bobble rows will alternate, one starting with 1 sc, and the other starting with 2 sc.

FYI: When working bobbles, they will pop out *away* from you, and therefore not be visible. This is why the bobble rows are listed as wrong side (ws) rows. Ironically, you will only see the bobbles when working the single crochet rows, or right side (rs) rows.

✕

HOOK
5.5 mm • US size I

YARN
Weight 4 • 550 yds
Lion Brand, Wool-Ease
Color: Natural Heather

OTHER TOOLS
Pillow insert (12" x 16")

GAUGE (4x4")

Front   Counting bobbles only:
        5½ stitches x 6½ rows

Back   Counting in sc:
        12 stitches x 16 rows

FINAL SIZE
Panel sizes, prior to assembly:

Front   Width: 16"
        Height: 12"

Back   Width: 15½"
        Height: 11¾"

PREFACE

The following stitches, techniques, and abbreviations are featured in this project.
Take a moment to review before starting.

▶ Video + material support: debrosse.com/moderncrochet

bo	bobble stitch / p. 158
ch	chain / p. 144
rep	repeat
sc	single crochet / p. 148
sl st	slip stitch / p. 146
st(s)	stitch(es)

FRONT

Front and back panels are worked in rows. Turning chain does not count as stitch.

Begin	Ch 50.
Row 1	Sc in 2nd ch from hook and in each ch across; ch 1, turn. (49)
Row 2 (ws)	Sc in first st, *bo in next st, sc in next st, rep from * in each st across; ch 1, turn. (49)
Row 3 (rs)	Sc in each st across; ch 1, turn. (49)
Row 4 (ws)	Sc in first 2 sts, *bo in next st, sc in next st, rep from * until 1 st remains, sc in last st; ch 1, turn. (49)
Row 5 (rs)	Sc in each st across; ch 1, turn. (49)

Rep rows 2–5 until 41 rows completed, or work measures 12 inches and ends on a rs row.
Omit the turning chain after final row. Cut yarn, and draw through loop on hook.

BACK

Begin	Ch 50.
Row 1	Sc in 2nd ch from hook and in each ch across; ch 1, turn. (49)
Row 2	Sc in each st across; ch 1, turn. (49)

Rep row 2 until 45 rows completed, or work measures 11¾ inches.
Omit the turning chain after final row. Cut yarn, and draw through loop on hook.

SEAM

A Hold both panels together with bobble side facing out.

B Pin panels together to align. Loosely sl st around perimeter of pillow (top, side, bottom). Top and bottom st counts will match up perfectly, while sides won't match stitch for stitch.

C Insert pillow form and stitch up 4th side.

Finish	Cut yarn, and draw through loop on hook. Tuck in ends.

THE GONAÏVES
FAUX FUR COWL

✕

Fur clothing has been around since the beginning of time, but not until recently could you crochet a faux fur accessory. With this faux fur yarn, the stitches completely disappear, allowing your final piece to look like a solid piece of fur.

Construction: As a general rule, when working with more texture-rich yarns, the stitch definition is greatly reduced, which means the overall shape of the finished piece will make more of a statement than the individual stitches that compose it. With this understanding, the Gonaïves cowl is made from a simple single crochet through both loops, but with a beautifully layered twist.

This cowl is worked in continuous rounds for a seamless finish. Normally when joining, it's imperative that you not twist your chain, but in this piece we'll intentionally twist it. By doing so, you'll crochet the cowl's twist right into the work without lifting a finger otherwise.

Because of the fluffiness of the fur, you're actually working a bit in the blind, in that you can't see your stitches. Use your fingers to graze over the stitches and find the next place to insert your hook. You'll quickly develop a new rhythm for this type of yarn, and enjoy the feel of the fur between your fingers.

✕

HOOK
11.5 mm • US size P

YARN
Weight 6 • 130 yds
Lion Brand, Go For Faux
Color: Baked Alaska

OTHER TOOLS
Darning needle

GAUGE
Not visible

FINAL SIZE
When laid flat, with the twist:
Width: 13"
Height: 13"

PREFACE

The following stitches, techniques, and abbreviations are featured in this project. Take a moment to review before starting.

 Video + material support: debrosse.com/moderncrochet

	continuous rounds / p. 26
ch	chain / p. 144
sc	single crochet / p. 148
sl st	slip stitch / p. 146
st(s)	stitch(es)

BODY

Scarf is worked in continuous rounds.
Do not join, chain, or turn between rounds.
There is no right or wrong side.

Begin	Ch 42; *twist* chain 360°, sl st to join.
Rounds 1–23	Sc in all sts around.
Finish	Cut yarn, and draw through loop on hook.
	Weave in ends.

THE ARNAUD
BASKET

×

I've never met a basket I didn't love, and the Arnaud Basket is no exception. I especially love the oversized scale of it, perfect for tossing in books, decorative throws, or the yarn stash.

Construction: To create a sturdy material, we'll work two pieces of yarn simultaneously, in a technique called double-stranding. Additionally, we'll go down a hook size. Together, this will create a denser fabric.

The base is worked in joined rounds, while the sides are worked in continuous rounds. I highly recommend placing a stitch marker in the first stitch of every round to keep your bearings. To transition from the base to the sides and establish an edge to the basket, we'll work that round in the back loop only.

Alterations: The basket can be made in any size and proportion. Here is how to adjust:

+ Narrower: Work fewer rounds on the base.
+ Wider: Work additional rounds on the base.
+ Shorter: Work fewer rounds on the sides.
+ Taller: Work additional rounds on the sides.

✕

HOOK
10 mm • US size N

YARN
Weight 6 • 550 yds
Lion Brand, Wool-Ease Thick & Quick
Color: Charcoal

OTHER TOOLS
Stitch marker (x2)
Darning needle

GAUGE (4x4")
6½ stitches x 7 rows

FINAL SIZE
Diameter of base: 14"
Height: 9"

PREFACE   The following stitches, techniques, and abbreviations are featured in this project. Take a moment to review before starting.

▶ Video + material support: debrosse.com/moderncrochet

	continuous rounds / p. 26
	double-stranded / p. 33
	joined rounds / p. 26
	magic ring / p. 162
blo	back loop only / p. 28
ch	chain / p. 144
inc	increase = work 2 sc in same stitch / p. 29
rep	repeat
sc	single crochet / p. 148
sl st	slip stitch / p. 146
st(s)	stitch(es)

A

B

BASE

Yarn is worked double-stranded for the entire project. The base is worked in joined rounds, by slip stitching into the first stitch. On each round, first single crochet goes into the same stitch as the join, last single crochet does not go into the slip stitch. To help identify stitches, place a stitch marker into first and last stitch of every round.

Begin	Create a magic ring. Ch 1.
Round 1	Sc 7 in ring; sl st to join, ch 1. (7)
Round 2	Inc in each st; sl st to join, ch 1. (14)
A **Round 3**	*Sc in next st, inc in next st; rep from * around; sl st to join, ch 1. (21)
Round 4	*Inc in next st, sc in next 2 sts; rep from * around; sl st to join, ch 1. (28)
Round 5	*Sc in next 3 sts, inc in next st; rep from * around; sl st to join, ch 1. (35)
Round 6	*Inc in next st, sc in next 4 sts; rep from * around; sl st to join, ch 1. (42)
Round 7	*Sc in next 5 sts, inc in next st; rep from * around; sl st to join, ch 1. (49)
Round 8	*Inc in next st, sc in next 6 sts; rep from * around; sl st to join, ch 1. (56)
Round 9	*Sc in next 7 sts, inc in next st; rep from * around; sl st to join, ch 1. (63)
Round 10	*Inc in next st, sc in next 8 sts; rep from * around; sl st to join, ch 1. (70)
Round 11	*Sc in next 9 sts, inc in next st; rep from * around; sl st to join, ch 1. (77)

SIDES

Sides are worked in continuous rounds.

B **Round 12**	Sc blo in each st around. (77)
Rounds 13–26	Sc through both loops in each st around. (77)
Finish	Cut yarn, and draw through loop on hook.
	Weave in ends.

THE TORBECK
BEANIE

✕

The Torbeck Beanie is one of my favorite designs. Crochet's Achilles' heel is that it often doesn't provide adequate stretch, and is often too bulky. This hat defies the odds, with both the perfect amount of stretch and lightweight crown shaping. It's a classic hat, no longer reserved only for the knitters.

Construction: This hat is worked lengthwise and is finished with a seam. It is worked entirely in slip stitch back loop only, and requires a loose tension.

When constructing a hat, it's integral that fewer stitches are used at the top (or crown) to minimize bulk. To do so in this hat, we'll use a unique technique called short rows. In short rows, you're simply leaving a few of the final stitches in that row unworked, and moving on to the next row as normal. When those unworked stitches are used later, you'll start to see your work come to life as the top of the hat naturally bends into a dome shape. After working all rows, you'll seam the ends together, and cinch the top closed.

Alterations: I went with a super classic pomless finish, but adding a pom is never a bad idea. For the color-block enthusiasts, consider starting the hat in one color and transitioning to the other midway (note that the color blocking will be left and right versus bottom and top).

✕

HOOK
7 mm

YARN
Weight 4 • 180 yds
Lion Brand, Wool-Ease
Color: Natural Heather

OTHER TOOLS
Darning needle

GAUGE (4x4")
14 stitches x 22 rows

FINAL SIZE
When laid flat, without brim fold:
Width: 7"
Height: 12½"

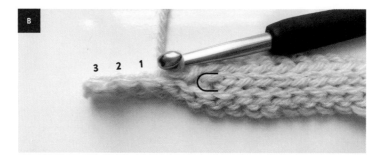

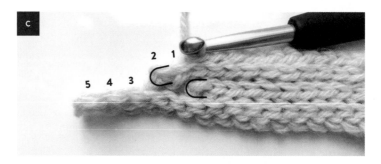

⊂ Indicates ends of previous sets of rows.
This is notated to help you keep your bearings.

PREFACE

The following stitches, techniques, and abbreviations are featured in this project.
Take a moment to review before starting.

▶ Video + material support: debrosse.com/moderncrochet

	back bump / p. 22
	short rows / p. 24
	whip stitch / p. 166
blo	back loop only / p. 28
ch	chain / p. 144
sl st	slip stitch / p. 146
st(s)	stitch(es)

BODY

Hat is worked lengthwise, in rows. Some rows are worked as short rows.
Turning chain does not count as a stitch.

	Begin	Ch 46.
	Row 1	Sl st into back bump in 2nd ch from hook and in each ch across; ch 1, turn. (45)
A	**Row 2**	Sl st blo in first 40 sts, leave remaining 5 sts unworked; ch 1, turn. (40)
	Row 3	Sl st blo each st across; ch 1, turn. (40)
B	**Row 4**	Sl st blo in first 40 sts, sl st blo next 2 sts (unworked sts from row 2), leave remaining 3 sts unworked; ch 1, turn. (42)
	Row 5	Sl st blo, all sts; ch 1, turn. (42)
C	**Row 6**	Sl st blo in first 40 sts, leave remaining 5 sts unworked; ch 1, turn. (40)
	Row 7	Sl st blo each st across; ch 1, turn. (40)
D	**Row 8**	Sl st blo in first 40 sts, sl st blo next 5 sts (unworked sts from previous rows); ch 1, turn. (45)
	Row 9	Sl st blo each st across; ch 1, turn. (45)

Repeat rows 2–9 ten times, or until work reaches 16 inches from row 1.

Finish	Omit the turning chain after final row.
	Cut yarn, and draw through loop on hook. Weave in ends.

SEAM

Whip stitch first and last rows together.
With new piece of 10" yarn, weave through crown of stitches, pull closed, tie off.
Weave in all ends.

THE VACHE
BOLSTER PILLOW

×

The curvature of the bolster pillow adds a soft touch to any piece of furniture. I designed this pattern in two finishes: a chunky unspun wool and a lush velvet. The unspun wool has rich stitch definition, while the velvet has an I-can't-stop-touching-this feel. Enjoy making one or both.

Construction: This pillow is totally seamless so that it has an effortlessly clean finish with no wrong side. To achieve this, all stitches are worked in the continuous round without any turning chains or slip stitch joins. We'll start by making a flat circle that increases each round, a tube shape with no size change, then finish with another flat circle that decreases in size. All work should be completed as normal, and *not* around the pillow, until the final section. I periodically placed the work on the pillow to confirm the size (and to be honest, I was just excited to see it come to life), but I found that my tension was too loose if I kept it on while working.

FYI: While the bolster pillow insert length is 16", the ends are pudgy, which means our work will actually measure longer than that, so no need to panic when the numbers seem off.

Alterations: Try out a longer or wider bolster pillow! For a longer pillow, work additional rows to the body of the work until you've reached the opposite end. For a wider pillow, work additional rounds on your endcaps, adding the appropriate increases (see p. 27).

✕

HOOK
10 mm • US size N

YARN
Weight 7 • 150 yds
Wool and the Gang, Crazy Sexy Wool
Color: Ivory White

OTHER TOOLS
Bolster pillow form (6" x 16")
Stitch marker
Darning needle

GAUGE (4x4")
5½ stitches x 6 rows

FINAL SIZE
Width: 6½"
Length: 18½"

PREFACE

The following stitches, techniques, and abbreviations are featured in this project. Take a moment to review before starting.

▶ Video + material support: debrosse.com/moderncrochet

	continuous rounds / p. 26
	magic ring / p. 162
blo	back loop only / p. 28
ch	chain / p. 144
dec	decrease = work 2 sc together / p. 29
inc	increase = work 2 sc in same stitch / p. 29
rep	repeat
sc	single crochet / p. 148
st(s)	stitch(es)

BOTTOM

Entire pattern is worked in the continuous round.
To help identify stitches, place a stitch marker into first stitch of every round.

	Begin	Create a magic ring. Ch 1.
A	**Round 1**	Sc 7 in ring. (7)
B	**Round 2**	Inc in each st around. (14)
	Round 3	*Sc in next st, inc in next st; rep from * around. (21)
	Round 4	*Inc in next st, sc in next 2 sts; rep from * around. (28)

BODY

Continue to work the body without yet inserting the pillow.

C	**Rounds 5-30**	Sc blo in each st around. (28)
D	Occasionally insert pillow form to check circumference fit. Adjust tension if necessary.	

TOP

E	Insert pillow form. Body should reach endcap seam of pillow form.

Work +/- rounds to achieve proper length before resuming pattern.
The following rounds seal the case around the pillow.

Round 31	*Dec in next 2 sts, sc in next 2 sts; rep from * around. (21)
Round 32	*Sc in next st, dec in next 2 sts; rep from * around. (14)
Round 33	Dec in next 2 sts around. (7)
Round 34	Sc in each st. (7)
	Cut yarn, and draw through loop on hook.
Finish (F)	Cut 12" piece of yarn and thread darning needle.
	Weave through final 7 stitches, pull closed, tie off. Tuck ends inside.

✕

HOOK
7 mm

YARN
Weight 5 • 422 yds
Bernat, Velvet
Color: Blackbird

OTHER TOOLS
Bolster pillow form (6" x 16")
Stitch marker
Darning needle

GAUGE (4x4")
8½ stitches x 9 rows

FINAL SIZE
Width: 6½"
Length: 18½"

The following stitches, techniques, and abbreviations are featured in this project. Take a moment to review before starting.

▶ Video + material support: debrosse.com/moderncrochet

	continuous rounds	/ p. 26
	double-stranded	/ p. 33
	magic ring	/ p. 162
ch	chain	/ p. 144
dec	decrease = work 2 sc together	/ p. 29
inc	increase = work 2 sc in same stitch	/ p. 29
rep	repeat	
sc	single crochet	/ p. 148
st(s)	stitch(es)	

BOTTOM

Entire pattern is worked in the continuous round, with double-stranded yarn. To help identify stitches, place a stitch marker into first stitch of every round. All figures reference p. 90 (note that figure C does not apply to this variation of the pattern).

	Begin	Create a magic ring. Ch 1.
A	**Round 1**	Sc 7 in ring. (7)
B	**Round 2**	Inc in each st around. (14)
	Round 3	*Sc in next st, inc in next st; rep from * around. (21)
	Round 4	*Inc in next st, sc in next 2 sts; rep from * around. (28)
	Round 5	*Sc in next 3 sts, inc in next st; rep from * around. (35)
	Round 6	*Inc in next st, sc in next 4 sts; rep from * around. (42)

BODY

Continue to work the body without yet inserting the pillow.

	Rounds 7–46	Sc in each st around. (42)
D		Occasionally insert pillow form to check circumference fit. Adjust tension if necessary.

TOP

E   Insert pillow form. Body should reach endcap seam of pillow form. Work +/- rounds to achieve proper length before resuming pattern. The following rounds seal the case around the pillow.

	Round 47	*Dec in next 2 sts, sc in next 4 sts; rep from * around. (35)
	Round 48	*Sc in next 3 sts, dec in next 2 sts; rep from * around. (28)
	Round 49	*Dec in next 2 sts, sc in next 2 sts; rep from * around. (21)
	Round 50	*Sc in next st, dec in next 2 sts; rep from * around. (14)
	Round 51	Dec in next 2 sts around. (7)
	Round 52	Sc in each st. (7)
		Cut yarn, and draw through loop on hook.
F	**Finish**	Cut 12" piece of yarn and thread darning needle.
		Weave through final 7 stitches, pull closed, tie off. Tuck ends inside.

THE LÉOGÂNE
INFINITY SCARF

✕

The Léogâne Infinity Scarf is named after the very first city I visited in Haiti, and the hometown of little DeBrosse himself (read more from my full adventure on p. 11). This is the very first pattern I wrote, and it remains a classic to this day. Its chunky, ribbed texture has both the perfect drape and all-of-the warmth. It wraps around twice, with no wrong side.

Construction: The Léogâne is constructed in joined turned rounds. This means that before each turning chain, we'll slip stitch into the first stitch of the row to join them. The final seam *will* be visible, but subtle. To achieve the ribbing effect, we'll use single crochets through the back loop only. Because the piece is getting turned each row, this will begin to create ridges. Note that no matter what row you're on, the back loop is always the farthest away from you.

Alterations: Consider doing the first half of the scarf in one color, and the second half in another. More of a traditional scarf than infinity scarf person? Rather than joining the work, do a normal turning chain and work in rows. A traditional scarf *does* need to be longer, so add more chains until you reach your desired length.

✕

HOOK
11.5 mm • US size P

YARN
Weight 6 • 212 yds
Lion Brand, Wool-Ease Thick & Quick
Color: Charcoal

OTHER TOOLS
Stitch marker (x2)
Darning needle

GAUGE (4x4")
7 stitches x 7 rows

FINAL SIZE
When laid flat:
Width: 29"
Height: 7½"

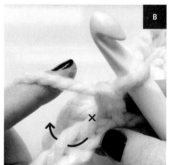

PREFACE

The following stitches, techniques, and abbreviations are featured in this project.
Take a moment to review before starting.

▶ Video + material support: debrosse.com/moderncrochet

	joined turned rounds / p. 26
beg	beginning
blo	back loop only / p. 28
ch	chain / p. 144
sc	single crochet / p. 148
sk	skip
sl st	slip stitch / p. 146
st(s)	stitch(es)

BODY

This scarf is worked in joined turned rounds. On each round, the first single crochet does *not* go into slip stitch, and last single crochet *does* go into the same stitch as the join. To help identify stitches, place a stitch marker into first and last stitch of every round.

Begin With loose tension, ch 88.
Sl st to first ch to join (careful not to twist); ch 1, *do not* turn.

Round 1 Sc in each ch around. (88)
 A Sl st through both loops of first st to join to beg of round; ch 1, turn.

Rounds 2–13 **B** Sk sl st, sc blo in each st around. (88)
Sl st through both loops of first st to join to beg of round; ch 1, turn.

Finish Omit the turning chain after final row.
Cut yarn, and draw through loop on hook. Weave in ends.

THE CÔTEAUX
TASSEL

✕

Tassels are like chocolate, pizza, and three-day weekends—you can't have enough. Did I need another tassel in my life when I designed this piece? No. But do I love it? Yes. My favorite part is that it takes on the characteristics of other crafts (looking at you, macramé), while being nothing more than a row of single crochets.

I've tested it on a doorknob, as a gift topper, as a gift itself, and draped around a bottle of Merlot, and I am happy to report it wins the room every time.

Construction: The tassel requires no materials other than the yarn itself. We will first cut the yarn into a bundle of individual pieces, and then work a row of single crochets *around* the middle of said bundle to create a plump top. We'll fold it in half, and wrap the yarn around the base to fold our row in half.

The bundle of yarn will stick out from the bottom of our work, and this is where we level-up our ability to think out of the box. The yarn for this project is very intentionally a multi-ply cotton yarn, which will allow us to run a comb through it to separate out the threads. This creates a full and swoon-worthy effect.

×

HOOK
2.75 mm • US size C

YARN
Weight 3 • 65 yds
We Are Knitters, Pima Cotton
Color: Natural

*If using an alternate, yarn must be
a multi-ply cotton.*

OTHER TOOLS
Sharp scissors
Hardcover book (9" tall, 1" thick)
Fine-tooth comb

GAUGE
8 stitches per inch

FINAL SIZE
Width: 3½"
Height: 9"

PREFACE

The following stitches, techniques, and abbreviations are featured in this project. Take a moment to review before starting.

▶ Video + material support: debrosse.com/moderncrochet

	slip knot / p. 142
sc	single crochet / p. 148
st(s)	stitch(es)

BODY

Tassel is worked as a single row. Use tight tension for a clean finish.

Begin

- **A**   Wrap yarn around book 90x, lengthwise. Cut bottom. *(Creates 90 20" pieces of yarn.)*
- **B**   Lay flat on table, starting 5" from the right.

Row 1

- Place slip knot on hook.
- **C**   Work 80 sc around bundle of yarn or until row of stitches measures 10".
- **D**   Cut yarn with 1yd tail, and draw through loop on hook.

Gather

- **E**   Bring both tassel ends together and wrap yarn 15-20x around base.
- **F**   Insert hook into wrap to pull tail end through, adding it to the tassel.

Finish

- **G**   Hold top taut, and run comb through ends. Iron to smooth, then trim ends for a blunt edge.

THE AQUIN
VELVET SCRUNCHIE

✕

You may not love the return of the scrunchie, but you will probably (definitely) enjoy making one (or one dozen). With its super quick work-up time, inexpensive materials, and easy giftability, there's so much to love. I recommend velvet yarn on this project (swoon) to give it the look of a solid fabric. If you're not feeling quite bold enough to wear it in your hair, it also makes a lovely little statement piece on the wrist.

Construction: The scrunchie design skips a chain foundation and, instead, builds right onto the hair tie, making sure its base has the perfect stretch. After a joined round of single crochets, we'll do a round of increases, packing three treble crochets into every stitch. These increases essentially create too many stitches for the work to sit flat, thus making the perfect ruffled finish.

Alterations: For a slightly less chunky scrunchie, swap your treble crochets for double crochets (and only chain 2 to begin round 2).

✕

HOOK
5.5 mm • US size I

YARN
Weight 5 • 30 yds
Bernat, Velvet
Color: Blackbird

OTHER TOOLS
Hair tie
Darning needle

GAUGE
4 stitches per inch

FINAL SIZE
4¾" diameter

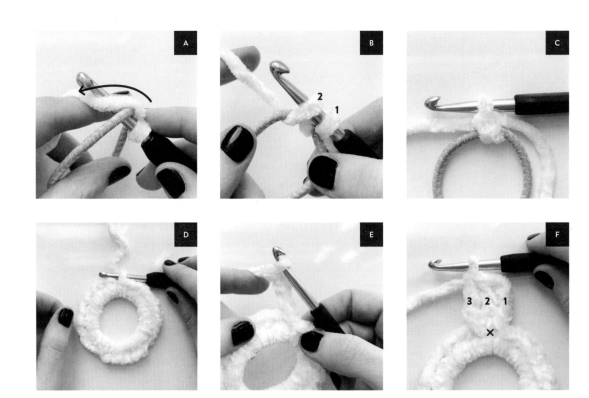

PREFACE

The following stitches, techniques, and abbreviations are featured in this project. Take a moment to review before starting.

▶ Video + material support: debrosse.com/moderncrochet

	joined rounds / p. 26
	slip knot / p. 142
ch, ch-	chain / p. 144
sc	single crochet / p. 148
sl st	slip stitch / p. 146
st(s)	stitches
tr	treble crochet / p. 154

BODY

Scrunchie is worked in joined rounds.
Turning chain counts as first treble crochet.

Begin	A	With slip knot on hook, place working yarn over hair tie.
	B	Draw up a loop from under the hair tie (2 loops on hook).
	C	Yarn over, draw through both loops on hook (this completes 1 sc).
Round 1	D	Work 24 more scs onto the hair tie, sl st to join.
Round 2	E	Ch 3 (counts as first tr), *do not* turn.
	F	Work 2 tr in same st as ch-3.
		Work 3 tr into each sc around, sl st to join. (72)
Finish		Cut yarn, and draw through loop on hook.
		Weave in ends.

THE LIMBÉ
LINEN SCARF

✕

The Limbé Linen Scarf marches to the beat of its own drum. Its texture resembles nothing of the granny square blanket that is so iconic of crochet. I designed this piece to be a bit oversized to truly celebrate that detail, so while I can't promise you'll finish it in a single sitting, I can promise that it'll be worth it. Identical textures show up on both sides, which means it'll style well every time.

Construction: This scarf is made from the linen stitch (also called moss or granite stitch), which is just a unique take on stitch *placement*, while still using only the basic skills and stitches. On each row, we'll work a repeat of single crochet (sc), then skip a stitch and just make a chain instead (sk st, ch 1). Each new row will then be staggered, so that our single crochets are above our chains, and our chains above our single crochets. *So now*, when we work our single crochets, we'll work them *around* the space created by the chain from the previous row with a technique called stitching into the ch-1 space. (To be clear: not *into* the chain, but *around* it entirely.)

I went with an unspun roving yarn on this project because its uniform finish really allows the texture of the linen stitch to be the hero.

✕

HOOK
6.5 mm • US size K 10½

YARN
Weight 5 • 465 yds
Patons, Alpaca Blend Yarn
Color: Birch

OTHER TOOLS
Darning needle

GAUGE (4x4")
12 stitches x 12 rows

FINAL SIZE
Width: 9"
Length: 70"

The following stitches, techniques, and abbreviations are featured in this project. Take a moment to review before starting.

▶ Video + material support: debrosse.com/moderncrochet

ch	chain / p. 144	
ch-sp	chain space / p. 28	
rep	repeat	
sc	single crochet / p. 148	
sk ch	skip chain / p. 28	
sk st	skip stitch / p. 28	
st(s)	stitch(es)	

BODY

Scarf is worked lengthwise, in rows. Turning chain counts as 1 stitch.

Begin	Ch 200.
Row 1	Sc in 4th ch from hook, *ch 1, sk 1 st, sc in next st; rep from * across row; ch 2, turn. (198)
Rows 2–26	Sc in first ch-sp, *ch 1, sk 1 sc, sc in next ch-sp; rep from * across row; ch 2, turn. (198)
Finish	Omit the turning chain after final row. Cut yarn, and draw through loop on hook. Weave in ends.

THE BAINET
THROW

×

The Bainet Throw is designed to be reversible, pairing a linear design with a more organic one. Both textures offer a classic finish, complemented by a bold twisted tassel.

Construction: The blanket is worked lengthwise. It uses a single crochet through the back loop only. The texture of this throw is only achieved when working all rows from the same side, meaning the work can't be flipped. In order to do so, we will start each row from a *new* piece of yarn (no turning chain or continuation from the previous row), using a technique called a standing stitch.

Every row should be completed on a single piece of yarn (no joining or ends to weave in), and leftovers are set aside for tassels. Starting over each row will create a sparse tassel effect that will be filled out at the end with additional yarn.

Alterations: For a longer blanket, chain additional stitches at the beginning. For a wider blanket, work additional rows. Note that final row count +1 (for the foundation chain), needs to be a multiple of four in order to complete tassels. If you're feeling fancy, consider changing yarn colors at certain rows to create a striped effect. Remember, you can always consult the gauge to review the exact width and height of stitches and rows.

✕

HOOKS
11.5 mm • US size P
5.5 mm • US size I *(for tassels only)*

YARN
Weight 6 • 954 yds
Lion Brand, Wool-Ease Thick & Quick
Color: Wheat

GAUGE (4x4")
6 stitches x 6 rows

FINAL SIZE
Not including tassels:
Width: 40"
Length: 58"

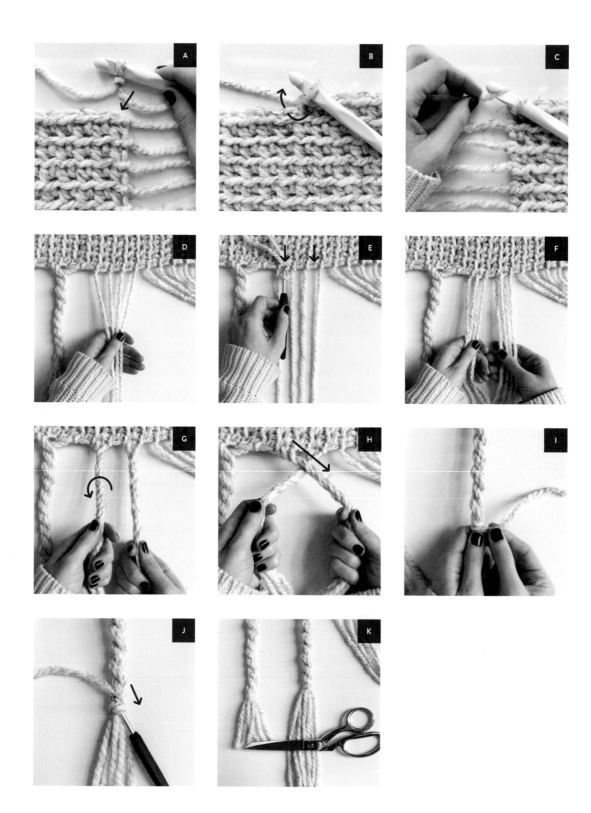

PREFACE

The following stitches, techniques, and abbreviations are featured in this project.
Take a moment to review before starting.

▶ Video + material support: debrosse.com/moderncrochet

	slip knot / p. 142
	standing stitch / p. 24
blo	back loop only / p. 28
ch	chain / p. 144
rs	right side
st(s)	stitch(es)
yo	yarn over / p. 141

BODY

Blanket is worked lengthwise with 11.5 mm hook. Each row begins with a standing stitch.
Work is never turned. Every row is worked on the right side with a new piece of yarn.

Begin   Leave 12" tail, place slip knot on hook, ch 90.
Cut 12" tail, yo to draw completely through loop on hook.

Pattern calls for back loops only, but row 1 will simply be worked into the ch sts.

Rows 1–59 (rs) **A** Leave 12" tail, place slip knot on hook.
B Work a standing sc blo in first st, work sc blo in each st across. (90)
C Cut 12" tail, yo to draw completely through loop on hook.

TASSELS

Cut 60 pieces of yarn, 24" each.
D Gather 4 consecutive tail ends.
E Use 5.5 mm hook to add one length of yarn after the first and third tail of your grouping.
F Separate out tail ends into 2 groups of 4.
G Twist each group, counterclockwise.
H Twist groups together, clockwise.
I Take 1 piece of tassel and wrap it around base of tassel three times.
J Insert 5.5 mm hook under the three wraps to pull end through and secure.
K Trim ends at 8".

THE VICTOIRE
WREATH

✕

Time is never more scarce than around the holidays, but this mini wreath project will make you feel like you can do it all. They work up in minutes, making them great gifts and effortless home decor.

Construction: The mini wreath is a made up of a single row of single crochets, worked around a wooden ring, then tied with a bow.

Alterations: This project leaves a lot of room for flexibility, and is written for a variety of ring sizes. To use a ring size not mentioned, simply add or subtract the number of single crochets in row 1 until your ring is thoroughly covered. Hook size corresponds to the yarn, so no need to change it with different ring sizes. You could even add a second row of stitches to the ring (just be sure to work 2 stitches into every stitch in order to increase properly).

✕

HOOK
5.5 mm • US size I

YARN
Weight 5 • 4 yds per wreath
Bernat, Maker Home Dec
Color: Cream

OTHER TOOLS
Wooden ring(s) in various sizes,
measured by outer diameter:

X-Small	1.6"
Small	2"
Medium	2.4"
Large	2.8"

GAUGE
3 stitches per inch

PREFACE

The following stitches, techniques, and abbreviations are featured in this project. Take a moment to review before starting.

▶ Video + material support: debrosse.com/moderncrochet

	slip knot / p. 142
sc	single crochet / p. 148
st(s)	stitches
yo	yarn over / p. 141

BODY

Wreath is worked in a single round.

Pattern is written for multiple sizes, showing stitch counts as follows: XS (S, M, L).

Photos feature a size L.

Begin

- **A** Leave 5" tail, place slip knot on hook, and place working yarn over ring.
- **B** Insert hook through center of ring, yo.
- **C** Pull up a loop (2 loops on hook).
- **D** Yo, pull through both loops on hook (this completes 1 sc).

Round 1

- **E** Work 14 (18, 19, 26) more scs onto wooden ring.
  Use +/- sts as necessary to completely cover the ring.
- **F** Shimmy sts together as you go.

Finish

- **G** Leave 5" tail, cut yarn, and draw through loop on hook.
- **H** Tie tails together in bow and trim.

THE JACMEL
BLANKET SCARF

✕

The Jacmel Blanket Scarf is a winter staple, acting like a statement piece, but feeling like your favorite blanket. It features a herringbone texture, which is relatively uncommon in crochet.

Construction: To achieve this herringbone texture, the Jacmel is worked in the continuous round. To avoid abrupt edges where the rounds start and end, the pattern calls for a little ramp-like stitch lineup, composed of stitches of varying heights. It looks complicated in writing, but conceptually it's quite simple. Note the relative heights of each stitch involved:

+ Herringbone half double crochet (hhdc) - Tall
+ Single crochet (sc) - Medium
+ Slip stitch (sl st) - Short

To begin the very first round, we'll work from the shortest to the tallest stitches, by working 2 sl st, then 2 sc, then proceeding into the hhdc. To end the final round, we'll work from the tallest to the shortest stitches, by finishing the final hhdc round, then working 2 sc, then 2 sl st before fastening off. In each instance, we'll see the ramp first grow, then shrink, and enjoy a flush edge.

✕

HOOK
15 mm • US size Q

YARN
Weight 6 • 424 yds
Lion Brand, Wool-Ease Thick & Quick
Color: Wheat

OTHER TOOLS
Darning needle

GAUGE (4x4")
5½ stitches x 4½ rows

FINAL SIZE
When laid flat:
Width: 40"
Height: 15"

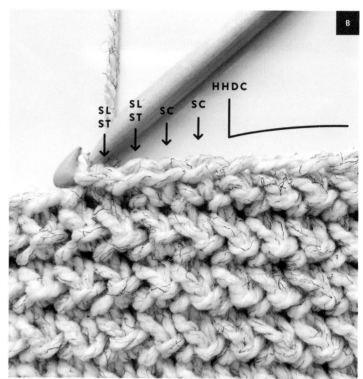

PREFACE

The following stitches, techniques, and abbreviations are featured in this project. Take a moment to review before starting.

▶ Video + material support: debrosse.com/moderncrochet

	continuous rounds / p. 26
ch	chain / p. 144
cont	continue
hhdc	herringbone half double crochet / p. 156
rem	remaining
sc	single crochet / p. 148
sl st	slip stitch / p. 146
st(s)	stitch(es)

BODY

Scarf is worked in continuous rounds.
Do not join, chain, or turn between rounds.

	Begin	Ch 110, sl st into first ch to join.
A	**Round 1**	Sl st in first 2 sts, sc in next 2 sts, hhdc in each rem st. (109)
	Rounds 2–19	Cont hhdc in each st around.
B	**Finish**	Sc in next 2 sts, sl st in next 2 sts.
		Cut yarn, and draw through loop on hook.
		Weave in ends.

138

STITCHES + SKILLS

INTRO

✕

Stitches are the building blocks of crochet. All crochet projects are made from a varied combination of stitches, paired with nuances that create visual differences, like working through a back loop only, or working in the round. The permutations are endless. In this section, I've detailed the step-by-step process of the basic stitches, plus a few fun ones. After you get a general idea of how stitches are built, you'll be able to learn new ones with ease.

In the following examples, all stitches are worked *in rows*, and worked through *both loops* (unless indicated otherwise). The textures created in these examples may look different from the texture of the pattern you're working, even though it's the same stitch. That is to be expected, as the nuances of the patterns (rows vs. rounds, back loop only vs. all loops, etc.) play a large role in determining the final texture. Regardless of the nuances, the stitches are worked the same.

▶ Video + material support: debrosse.com/moderncrochet

Before diving in, here are a few definitions to know:

WORKING YARN

The working yarn refers to the portion of the yarn that is coming *from* the main source (skein, ball, cake), rather than the tail end or yarn used in the project so far.

TAIL END

The tail end refers to the very tip of the yarn from which you'll start working, as opposed to the portion of the yarn that is coming *from* the main source (skein, ball, cake).

YARN OVER (YO)

Yarning over is a technique used in every stitch, and can be done any number of times. To yarn over (yo), bring the working yarn from the back to the front (toward you), going *over* the hook.

LOOP ON HOOK

The hook is (almost) always connected to the work by having a loop on it. This means that going into any stitch, and after finishing any stitch, one loop should remain. It is always counted as a loop on your hook, but never counted as a stitch.

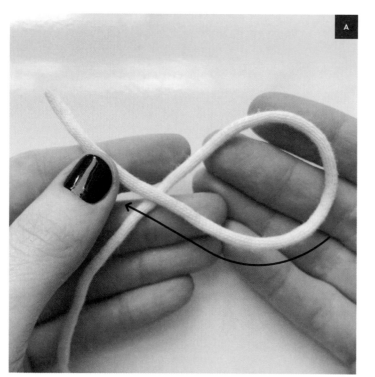

SLIP KNOT

×

OVERVIEW

The slip knot is a technique used to attach the yarn to your hook. This is the very first step of *any* pattern. The remaining tail will be woven in at the end of every project, so be sure to leave at least 4".

STEPS

A Cross tail end of yarn over working yarn.

B Reach fingers through, grab working yarn.

C Pull through loop.

D This completes the slip knot.

E Place on hook, adjust size to fit. The knot should be firmly attached, but loose enough to slide.

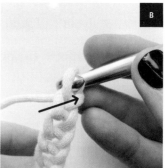

CHAIN (CH)

×

OVERVIEW

A chain is most often used to build the foundation of a crochet project (quantity of chains is relative to project size), or when working a turning chain between rows (quantity of chains is relative to stitch height). Note that whenever you see the abbreviation for chain (ch) appended with a hyphen (e.g., ch-sp), it is a noun and not a verb, meaning no stitches are worked, they are simply referenced.

Tip: When working a foundation chain, it's important that these are made in a loose tension since they have no stretch. A tight foundation chain may result in a taut edge.

STEPS

A Yarn over.

B Rotate hook to pull yarn through one loop on hook.
This completes 1 ch.

C When counting chains, never include the loop on your hook or the slip knot.

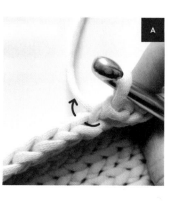

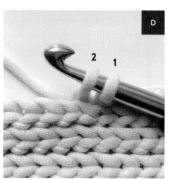

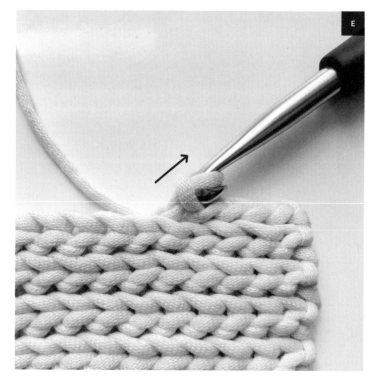

SLIP STITCH
(SL ST)

×

OVERVIEW

The slip stitch is most often used to join rounds, but can also be used for an entire row or round itself. It is the most minimal of stitches, with a very short height. When worked in back loop only (blo), as shown here, it creates a texture that looks knitted.

Tip: When working the slip stitch as a row or round, rather than as a join, tension is *everything*. When it's done too tight, the work will begin to shrink. When in doubt, make your slip stitches far looser than you feel comfortable.

STEPS

A For sl st blo, locate back loop.

B Insert hook through back loop of next st.

C Yarn over.

D Pull yarn through to draw up a loop, tilting your hook slightly up in order to enlarge loop 2 (2 loops on hook).

E Pull loop 2 through loop 1.

This completes 1 sl st.

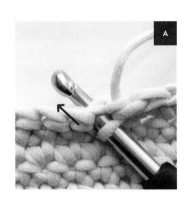

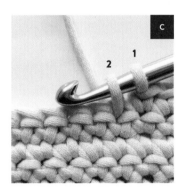

SINGLE CROCHET (SC)

×

OVERVIEW

The single crochet is one of the most basic but widely used crochet stitches. It creates a flat, dense fabric when worked through both loops. It is the building block of the half double crochet, double crochet, and treble crochet.

➕ **Tip:** For a better drape and a bit more visual interest, work the single crochet through the back loop only.

STEPS

A Insert hook in next st, going under both loops (unless pattern specifies front or back loop only).

B Yarn over.

C Pull yarn through stitch to draw up a loop (2 loops on hook).

D Yarn over, again.

E Pull yarn through both loops on hook.

This completes 1 sc.

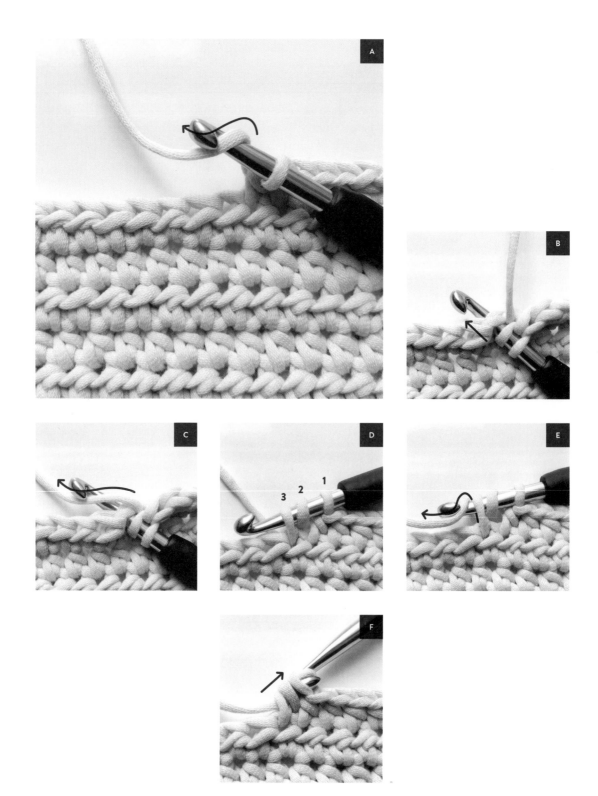

HALF DOUBLE CROCHET (HDC)

×

OVERVIEW

The half double crochet is a variation of the single crochet, and simply utilizes an additional yarn over. It has a bit more height than the single crochet, allowing projects to work up slightly quicker and with a bit more drape.

STEPS

A   Yarn over.

B   Insert hook in next stitch.

C   Yarn over.

D   Pull yarn through stitch to draw up a loop (3 loops on hook).

E   Yarn over.

F   Pull through all 3 loops on hook.

This completes 1 hdc.

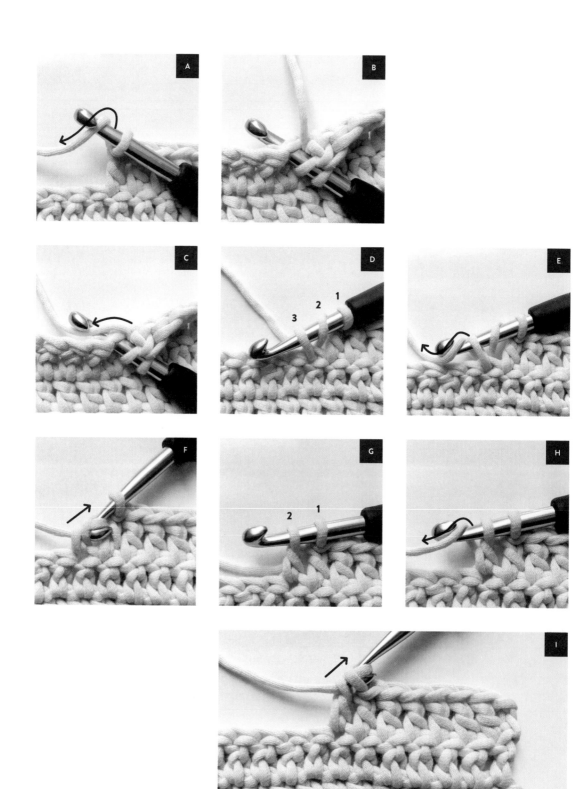

DOUBLE CROCHET (DC)

×

OVERVIEW

The double crochet is very similar to the half double crochet, but includes a third yarn over to create a greater height to the stitch.

STEPS

A Yarn over.

B Insert hook in next stitch.

C Yarn over.

D Pull yarn through stitch to draw up a loop (3 loops on hook).

E Yarn over.

F Pull through first 2 loops on hook.

G (2 loops on hook.)

H Yarn over.

I Pull through remaining 2 loops on hook.

This completes 1 dc.

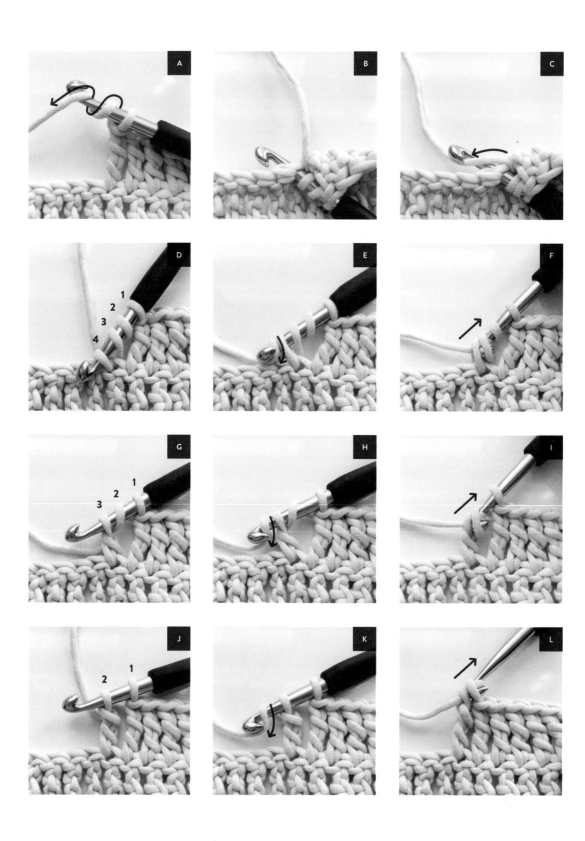

TREBLE CROCHET (TR)

×

OVERVIEW

The treble crochet works much like the double, but begins with a *double* yarn over. It is quite tall and works up quickly.

STEPS

A Yarn over, twice.

B Insert hook in next stitch.

C Yarn over.

D Pull yarn through stitch to draw up a loop (4 loops on hook).

E Yarn over.

F Pull through first 2 loops on hook.

G (3 loops on hook.)

H Yarn over.

I Pull through first 2 loops on hook.

J (2 loops on hook.)

K Yarn over.

L Pull through remaining 2 loops on hook.

This completes 1 tr.

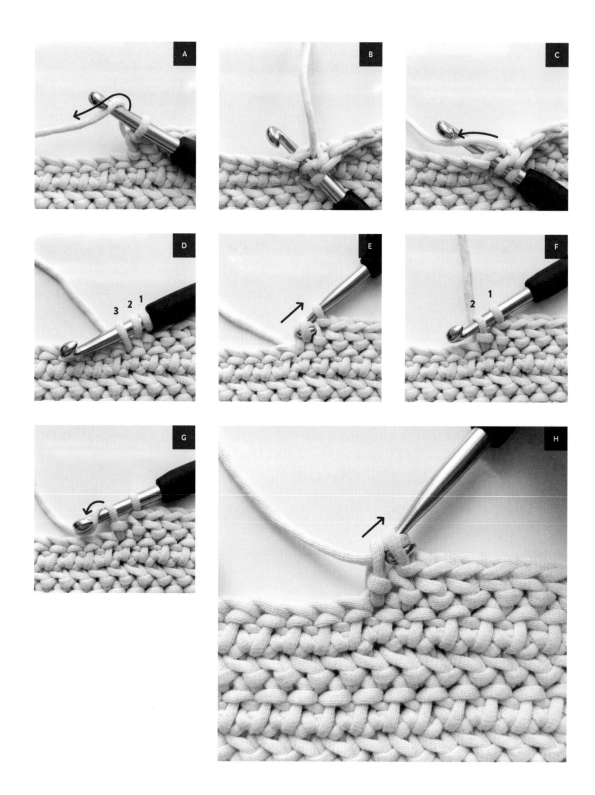

HERRINGBONE HALF DOUBLE CROCHET (HHDC)

×

OVERVIEW

The herringbone half double crochet is a combination of the half double crochet and a slip stitch. It is a rather uncommon stitch, despite being composed of basic elements. It creates an incredibly rich texture with a beautiful slant.

⊕ **Tip:** This stitch comes to life when worked in the round.

STEPS

A Yarn over.

B Insert hook in next stitch.

C Yarn over.

D Pull yarn through stitch to draw up a loop (3 loops on hook).

E Twist hook to slip loop 3 under loop 2.

F (2 loops on hook.)

G Yarn over.

H Pull through remaining 2 loops on hook.

This completes 1 hhdc.

BOBBLE STITCH (BO)

✕

OVERVIEW

Prior to working the bobble stitch, I recommend mastering the double crochet (see p. 152).

The bobble is created by working 5 double crochets into the same stitch, but rather than finishing each individual double crochet, the final yarn over and pull through is completed on all 5 at once. This creates a bulge in the work, known as a bobble. This bobble will pop away from you as you work.

Patterns will vary, but oftentimes bobbles are separated by a chain or single crochet to space them out. Because bobbles only show up on one side of the work, they are usually worked on alternate rows so that they are all facing the same direction. Depending on the pattern (and specifically, the stitches that precede the bobbles), they can stack directly above one another (as is the case with the Les Cayes Wall Hanging, p. 44), or they can stagger (as is the case with the Belladère Bobble Pillow, p. 62).

STEPS (SEE NEXT PAGE)

A   Yarn over.

B   Insert hook in next stitch.

C   Yarn over.

D   Pull yarn through stitch to draw up a loop (3 loops on hook).

E   Yarn over.

F   Pull through first 2 loops on hook.

G   This completes first dc (2 loops on hook).

H   Yarn over. This begins next dc.

I   Insert hook in *same* stitch.

J   Yarn over.

K   Pull through to draw up a loop (4 loops on hook).

L   Yarn over.

M   Pull through first 2 loops on hook.

N   (3 loops on hook.)

O   Continue working steps H-M until 6 loops on hook.*

P   Yarn over.

Q   Pull through all 6 loops.

R   This completes 1 bo (shown from right side).

Note that when counting loops, your hook always has a loop on it, so you're going to ADD 5 loops to your hook (therefore, 6 loops on your hook represents 5 dc).

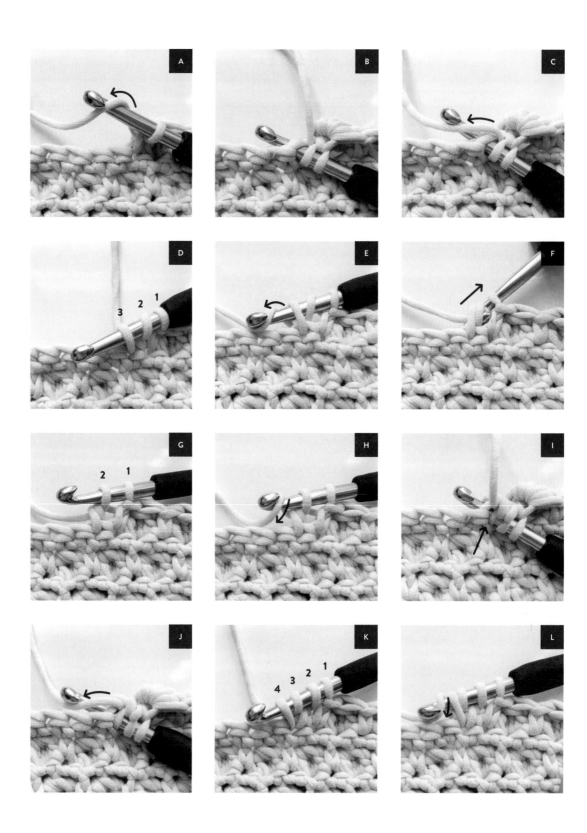

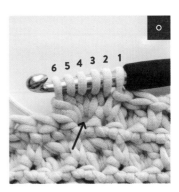

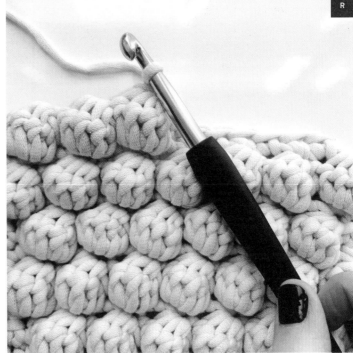

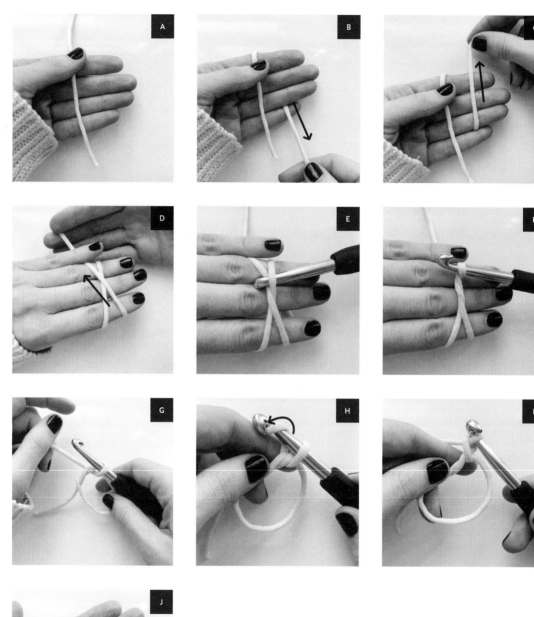

MAGIC RING

×

OVERVIEW

The magic ring, sometimes called the magic circle, or magic loop, is a technique used to start a project in the round. The magical aspect of the ring is that it has a slip knot effect in that can be pulled taut after the first row of stitches is worked into it.

STEPS

A Place yarn tail between thumb and fingers.

B Wrap working yarn behind hand, then back to front between ring finger and pinky.

C Wrap yarn across fingers, and begin to rotate hand to face palm down.

D Cross yarn *over* existing yarn to create an X.

E Insert hook *under* top right of X, and *over* top left of X. Rotate hook down to grab yarn.

F Pull through and twist to draw up a loop.

G Take ring off hand.

H Yarn over.

I Pull through to draw up a loop. This creates 1 ch.

J This completes the magic ring and first chain.

To work the first round of stitches into the magic ring, continue to the next page.

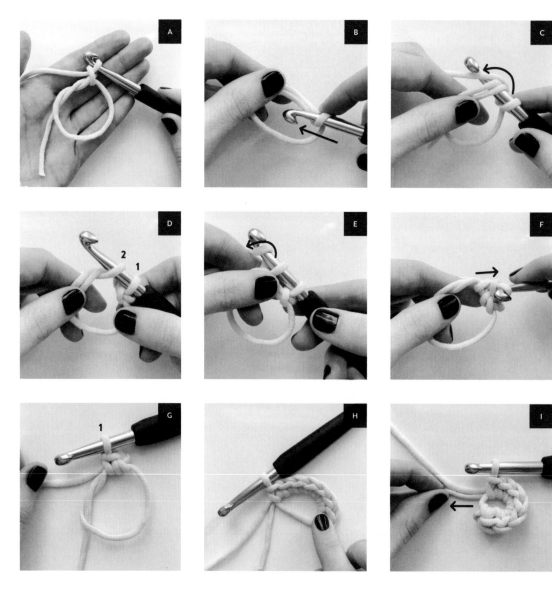

SC INTO A
MAGIC RING

×

OVERVIEW

After creating a magic ring, a pattern will indicate how many stitches to work *into* that ring. These stitches are worked over both the strand of the ring and the tail. It could be any type of stitch, and any number of stitches. In this example, we'll follow the common instruction: Sc 7 in ring.

STEPS

A First, create magic ring (see previous page).

B Insert hook into ring.

C Yarn over.

D Pull yarn through to draw up a loop (2 loops on hook).

E Yarn over.

F Draw through both loops on hook.

G This completes 1 sc.

H Continue working number of stitches instructed by pattern.

I Pull tail end of magic ring to tighten.

J This completes first round of stitches worked into magic ring. Proceed to next round of pattern.

WHIP STITCH

✕

OVERVIEW

The whip stitch is worked with a darning needle, rather than a crochet hook. It is less a stitch, and more of a technique for seaming panels or edges together. A pattern will indicate which panels to seam and how to properly align them. In this example, I'm using a contrasting color to distinguish the whip stitch from the work.

● **Tip:** Match up stitches evenly for the most subtle seam. Keep a consistent tension that is not too tight or too loose.

A **STEPS**

Thread darning needle with matching yarn.

Insert needle through both panels, in corresponding stitches.

Bring yarn and needle back *over* the work.

Insert through *next* 2 stitches, working in the same direction.

Continue to end.

Cut yarn and weave end through work.

CREDITS

THANK YOU

✕

One year, 170+ pages, 10,000+ photos, 5,568 yards of yarn, 32 status calls, 10 pattern testers, 6 black manicures, 5 cities, 3 all-book-files-got-deleted-nightmares, 2 little Haitian boys that I do not yet know, and an army of people made this book possible.

THE DREAM TEAM

PAIGE TATE & CO

It has been a total honor to work with the Paige Tate team. This book would not be possible without your support of the DeBrosse brand, and your desire to see it flourish in a new way. Alicia Brady, thank you for being a continued voice of encouragement, understanding, and enthusiasm. Clare Whitehead, thank you for the steadfast effort to get my work into the hands of makers. Peter Licalzi, thank you for always going the extra mile like it's your first. Brenna Licalzi, thank you for all the behind-the-scenes work that laid the foundation and path for the success of this book. Stephanie Carbajal, thank you for the incredible edit. Thank you all, for sharing your gifts and talents with me so generously.

EMILY REITER

From one perfectionist to another, I can't thank you enough for your continued investment in ensuring the accuracy of this book. Your eagle eye, wisdom, and attention to detail have been an invaluable gift to me. I also want to preemptively thank you on behalf of everyone who has been able to successfully complete a project from this book.

PATTERN TESTERS

I would not be able to confidently share my patterns with the world if they didn't first have your stamp of approval. Thank you for generously sharing your time, talents, and feedback with me. Angie Bivins, Mary Englar, Diana Friedenzohn, Melissa Georges, Emi Goh, Nadir Lawrence, Caitlyn McDuffie, Autumn Toland, Geneva Vasquez...I'm so grateful to be in this community with you.

PHOTOGRAPHERS

ALEXANDRA TAVEL + NICK HOGE

They don't come as patient, talented, or generous as the two of you. Your styling and photography brought this book to life in a way I could have only dreamed. I am honored to have had you on my team in this project, and will forever be grateful for the way you invested in this book like it was your very own.

ASHLEY + BRIAN WINTON

Thank you for so generously sharing your beautiful corner of upstate New York. Scraggly Pine Cabin, and all it's exquisite details, gave this book a voice it would not have had otherwise. Your creativity and thoughtfulness will go on to inspire others, and I hope it returns to you, tenfold.

FRIENDS + FAMILY

STEVEN CARTER

Bugs, I'm not crying, you are. This book should have *your* name on the cover. You were an unending source of support, encouragement, and grace, and this book would not be possible without you. Thank you for learning far more about crochet than you ever hoped to know, listening to (quite possibly) the most detail-laden daily book status recaps, and for all the many ways you quietly sacrificed to help me pursue my dream. You were my strength, confidence, and joy when I fell short. You believed in me from the very beginning, and every shaky moment in between. And here we are. *We* did it!

MARIE CUNNINGHAM

Hi, mom! Did you ever think we'd end up chatting here? Me either. I couldn't be more grateful to share this hobby with you. Thank you for making that first blanket for me when I was little, and then teaching me how to make blankets for others. I love sharing every bit of this journey with you, and already look forward to the blankets I know you'll be making for the boys.

ASHLEIGH KISER + ALEXANDRA TAVEL

First things first: #sorryforallthequestions. Thank you for being so generous with your crochet knowledge, and for the countless ways you continue to invest in my work. Thank you for being great colleagues, and even greater friends.

EMILY REASOR + LINDSEY SWEDICK

If I took you out to brunch for every time you checked in on me and the book, do you think we could single-handedly keep Bubby's in business? I can't imagine having pulled off this book without your support and encouragement. Thanks for being the best pals ever.

YARN + RESOURCE SUPPORT

CRAFT YARN COUNCIL

A huge thanks to Craft Yarn Council for your impeccable curation of crochet standards, resources, and guidelines. The community as a whole is stronger because of your work. Thank you for making it so generously available to us.

craftyarncouncil.com

LION BRAND

An admittedly sappy thank you to the team at Lion Brand, for making the very first yarn I ever crocheted with, to generously providing yarn support for my very first book. I would choose Wool-Ease Thick & Quick over chocolate if need be, and I could not have had more fun working with Go For Faux. Your products have been instrumental in the success of DeBrosse, and I am forever grateful.

lionbrand.com

WOOL AND THE GANG

Thank you to the talented folks at Wool and the Gang, for leading the charge on modern, innovative, and thoughtful crafting. Your wool is the stuff of dreams, and I am so grateful to have been able to use it in this book. Thank you for your continued investment and support in DeBrosse.

woolandthegang.com

YARNSPIRATIONS

Thank you to the generous team at Yarnspirations, for providing a beautiful range of yarn for this book. Your Bernat Velvet is to die for, Patons Alpaca is a total hero, and Bernat Maker Home Dec is a classic that I cannot work without. Thank you for elevating the work of makers everywhere.

yarnspirations.com

ABOUT THE
AUTHOR

×

Teresa Carter lives in New York City with her husband, soon to be joined by the two little boys they are adopting from Haiti. She is the founder and creator of DeBrosse, a full-service knitwear brand. She has sold over 200,000 crochet and knit patterns to date. Her designs have been featured by Martha Stewart, West Elm, House Beautiful, and more. Teresa leads a Masterclass, empowering other makers to build careers in the crochet and knit industry.

DEBROSSE.COM • @DEBROSSE_NYC

#MYMODERNCROCHET